Columbia Highlands

Exploring Washington's
Last Frontier

Text by Craig Romano

Photos by James Johnston

Published by Conservation Northwest with The Mountaineers Books
With a generous grant from Campion Foundation

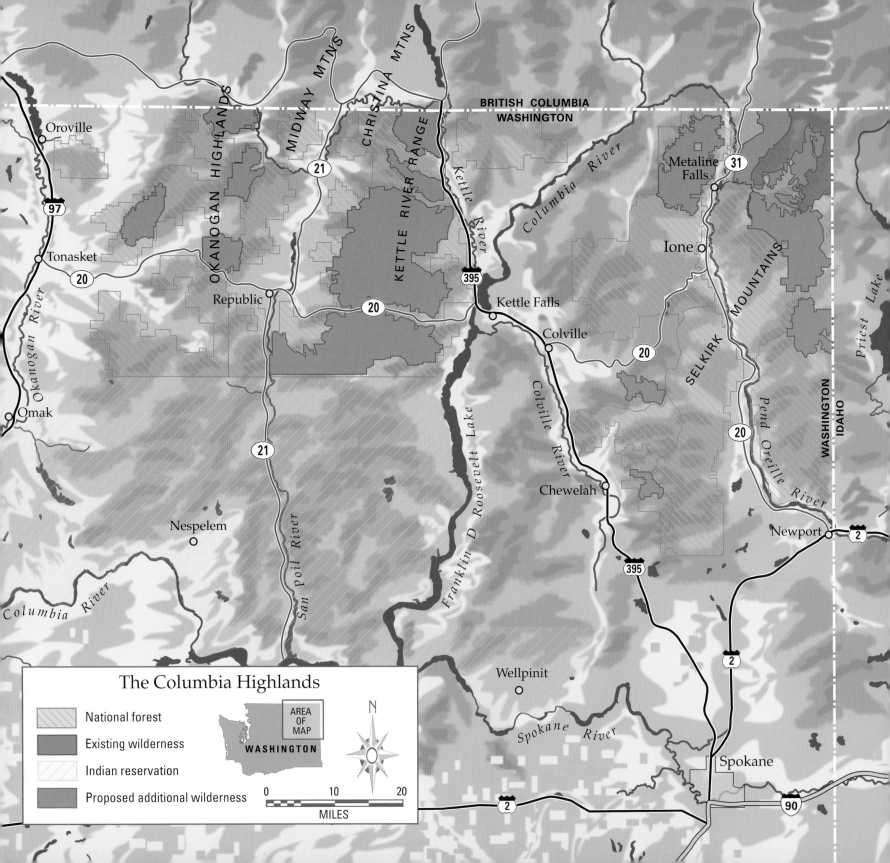

The Columbia Highlands

National forest	
Existing wilderness	
Indian reservation	
Proposed additional wilderness	

AREA OF MAP

WASHINGTON

N

0   10   20
MILES

Oroville

97

Tonasket

20

Okanogan River

Omak

OKANOGAN HIGHLANDS

MIDWAY MTNS

21

Republic

CHRISTINA MTNS

KETTLE RIVER RANGE

Kettle River

20

395

21

San Poil River

Nespelem

Columbia River

Franklin D Roosevelt Lake

BRITISH COLUMBIA
WASHINGTON

Columbia River

Kettle River

395

Kettle Falls

Colville

Colville River

Chewelah

395

Wellpinit

Spokane River

Metaline Falls

31

Ione

SELKIRK MOUNTAINS

20

Pend Oreille River

20

Priest Lake

WASHINGTON
IDAHO

Newport

2

2

Spokane

2

90

Contents

A Timeless
Treasure in a
Growing State

EAST OF THE CRAGGY and glacier-covered Cascade Mountains and north of the arid Columbia Plateau lies Washington's Columbia Highlands. The Selkirk Mountains and the Kettle River Range, which rise to heights exceeding seven thousand feet, are the highlands' impressive and imposing landmarks. But it is not the lofty peaks that attract most visitors here; it is the region's pure wildness and the rugged character of its local residents and communities that are so alluring.

A far cry from the bustling Puget Sound, time moves slowly here. Vestiges of the past are prevalent, and little of this land has been exploited and manipulated. Hundreds of miles of trails traverse these mountains, yet rarely are fellow hikers encountered on them.

The Columbia Highlands are a land of incredible biological diversity, where east meets west in the Evergreen State. A transition zone between the wet Cascades and the drier Rocky Mountains, the highlands act as a land bridge for wildlife populations from these greater ecosystems. Moose, lynx, and bighorn sheep, species more associated with the Rockies, thrive here. This land is a refuge for mountain caribou, grizzly, wolves, and wolverines. Flora mingles in this ecological conversion zone. Sagebrush creeps skyward on south slopes, while north-facing ravines shade dense stands of moisture-loving fir and cedar.

The human history is just as rich as its wildlife and forests. The independent spirit of the Wild West still thrives here, along with a strong sense of community. People continue to make a living off the land, not just through resource extraction, but through stewardship and recreation. To the Colville Nation, whose ancestors lived off this land for thousands of years, these mountains are sacred, a place where the spirit of the mountains can be felt in winds whistling through silver snags and in thunderous clouds swirling over high peaks aimed toward the heavens.

◄ Western larch provide autumn splendor in the Kettle River Range.
Photo © Craig Romano

◄◄ Sunset from Sherman Pass

At the Foot of the Rockies

The moon rises above snow-caked subalpine firs on Snow Peak.

Photo © Jasmine Minbashian

◄ The sky ignites at sunset in the Selkirk Mountains.

Photo © Eric Zamora

Spanning from the Okanogan River to Idaho, and framed by the Canadian border to the north and the Columbia Plateau to the south, the Columbia Highlands are a sprawling region that encompasses the northeast corner of Washington State. Part of the natural province known as the Okanogan Highlands, the Columbia Highlands consist primarily of two main mountain ranges that line the Columbia River as it enters Washington from British Columbia.

West of the Columbia, the Kettle River Range runs north to south for approximately seventy-five miles. Corralled by the Kettle River in the north and northeast, the Columbia in the east and south, and the San Poil River in the west, the Kettles form an imposing wall across the western highlands.

The eastern half of the Columbia Highlands contains the Selkirk Mountains. They also run north to south, but unlike the Kettles, which consist of a single, high crest with radiating ridges, the Selkirks are composed of parallel subranges. Bordered by the Columbia River to the west and the Spokane River to the south, the range's

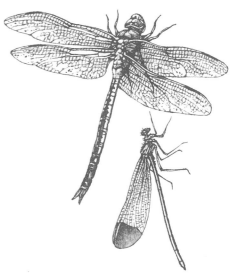

 Dragonfly and damselfly

eastern reaches in Washington are bisected by the Pend Oreille River. The Selkirks extend eastward into the Idaho Panhandle and northward into British Columbia, where they become increasingly craggier and higher. But they're impressive in the Columbia Highlands, too. Here, Gypsy Peak and Abercrombie Mountain exceed 7300 feet, the highest summits in eastern Washington.

Both the Kettle and Selkirk ranges are part of the Rocky Mountains. In the highlands they form the transitional zone between interior ranges and the coastal Cascades. And like all transitional zones, the Columbia Highlands are rich in biological diversity.

From the 7140-foot summit of Copper Butte, a former lookout site on the highest peak in the Kettle River Range, look in any direction and a little-known but complex landscape of ridges, valleys, forests, and rivers is revealed. South along the rounded, lofty Kettle Crest is an alpine world of golden lawns and emerald canopies streaked

 A pair of coyotes
Photo © Paul Bannick

 ▶ Sagebrush mingles with subalpine fir on the east slope of Columbia Mountain.

Douglas-fir, ponderosa pine, and a ground
cover of heart-leaved arnica (*Arnica cordifolia*)

◄ Sunset from Copper Butte

with stands of silver snags. To the north are more jumbled peaks shrouded in thick forests, punctuated with patches of meadows that in summer are bursting with blossoming wildflowers. Trace the lumpy spine of the Kettle Crest as it fades into British Columbia. From the Canadian hinterlands emerges an unrestrained Kettle River that slices a crescent across flaxen fields and then retreats into the nation of its birth before wrapping around the mountains that bear its name and reentering the Evergreen State.

Now cast your attention westward over spacious valleys carved by retreating glaciers of another era. The Christina and Midway mountains, resilient outposts of broad peaks cloaked in conifers, hover above the rolling countryside, lonely sentinels of Washington's forgotten northeast corner.

A sea of peaks crowds the eastern horizon. Follow the prevailing winds as they roll across this landscape, and note that the greens of the rippling ranges grow darker. As storm clouds from the west migrate eastward, each subsequent uplift wrings out a little more rainfall. Shadows cast on the surrounding glens grow darker, too. The ridges rise progressively higher, culminating in a tight cluster of rugged peaks in the far northeast.

And if you continue to face the direction to where the sun makes its first appearance, you may see its warming light sparkle off waters a vertical mile below. Splicing this land of broad valleys, rolling hills, and rugged peaks is the lifeline of the Pacific Northwest: the Columbia River. On its wayward journey from the ice fields of the Canadian Rockies to the crashing surf of the Pacific, the mighty Columbia enters Washington State here through a gateway flanked by the Selkirk Mountains and the Kettle River Range. Before snaking across the channeled scablands and through the Cascade Mountains, the powerful river must first flow through the wild and varied landscape of the Columbia Highlands.

Much of this little-known country is within the public domain, open to hikers, equestrians, hunters, anglers, and wildlife enthusiasts. The United States Forest Service manages over one million acres of this remote corner of Washington through the Colville National Forest and parts of the Okanogan and Kaniksu national forests. The United States Fish and Wildlife Service administers another 40,000 acres, while the Washington Department of Natural Resources oversees more than 220,000 acres. Within this mosaic of public lands, large tracts of old-growth forest and rugged parcels unmarred by roads and development still exist. And within these pockets of wild lands, some of Washington's rarest residents hang on to survival. The Columbia Highlands provide habitat for such endangered and threatened species as the grizzly bear, mountain caribou, lynx, wolf, and wolverine. Yet, while the Columbia Highlands contain some of the most beautiful, remote, and wildlife-rich lands in Washington, less than 3 percent of these public lands are classified as federal wilderness. Just one small wilderness area of forty-one thousand acres—the Salmo-Priest Wilderness—is all that has been set aside from the ever-present and growing threats of road construction, resource exploitation, and off-road vehicles.

For decades the Columbia Highland's best protection was its obscurity. But as Washington's population continues to burgeon, pressure is mounting to open up these wild lands to development and other incompatible uses. How we respond to these impending threats depends on how much we really cherish and value this special place.

Bobcat
Photo © Paul Bannick

▶ Fire-dependent ponderosa pine forests dominate the lower valleys of the Kettle River Range.

Washington's Last Great Place

The Columbia Highlands boast a high diversity of butterfly species, including the western tiger swallowtail butterfly.

Photo © Alan Bauer

◄ Looking south to the Colville Indian Reservation, from Thirteenmile Mountain

Photo © Jasmine Minbashian

State Route 20 twists and curves across the Columbia Highlands. The only major road to traverse the region from west to east, it is often void of traffic. Undulating between deep valleys and broad, open uplands, SR 20 reaches its pinnacle crossing the Kettle Crest, the lofty backbone of the Kettle River Range, at Sherman Pass. From this 5575-foot mountain gap, the highest highway pass in the state, are views of a countryside that appears uninhabited.

Along the highway's 175-mile journey from Tonasket to Newport, its largest settlement, Colville, contains fewer than six thousand inhabitants. But this little city, the administrative seat of Stevens County, is undeniably the metropolitan center of the region. A bustling community rooted in forest products manufacturing, Colville also supports a thriving commercial sector. And while big-box retailers and fast-food franchises dot the two main roads leading into the city, Colville remains fairly compact. Its downtown area emanates a 1950s charm. The pace is unhurried. The streets are welcoming. It is a long way from Seattle.

West of Colville lies Ferry County. Named for Elisha Ferry, first governor of the state of Washington, this county of 1.4 million acres is home to just over 7600 residents, only 3000 more than when the county was first formed in 1899. There is not one traffic light in the entire county, and no fast-food, motel, or retail franchises, either. Republic, the largest community and civic heart of Ferry County, still shows its pioneer-mining roots. The town is quiet except during hunting season, when hundreds of orange-clad hunters jam its hotels, stores, and taverns.

The eastern reaches of the Columbia Highlands lie within Pend Oreille County, Washington's newest county, having split from Stevens County in 1911. Pend Oreille's nine hundred thousand-plus acres are home to just 12,500 people. Like jewels on a necklace, its handful of communities are strung along the Pend Oreille River, lifeblood of the county. Newport, county seat and center of commerce, is the largest community. Metaline Falls is the most charming, a once-dusty concrete manufacturing town that now supports a thriving arts community.

In the Columbia Highlands, deer outnumber people. Moose wander out on deserted roads. Drivers slow down to wave to and acknowledge each other. Cattle still dominate the sprawling pastures of the valleys. The mountains are thickly forested, and, while clear-cuts aren't absent, McMansions marring their high slopes are. In the Columbia Highlands, vestiges of the old Northwest are everywhere.

In the past century, change has been slow here. Although fur traders, missionaries, and surveyors first traveled through the area two hundred years ago, it wasn't until the turn of the last century that settlement flourished. Newly discovered mineral wealth, expansive rangelands, and a seemingly infinite timber base attracted pioneers and opportunity seekers to the region.

And while two of the area's great rivers, the Columbia and Pend Oreille, have been harnessed to power the ever-expanding Puget Sound metropolitan area—their rapids subdued, their floodplains inundated, and their wild spirits broken—the Kettle River flows freely. From its source high in the Monashee Mountains of British Columbia, the Kettle tumbles and churns and slithers through lazy oxbows for over two hundred

Common camas, nodding onion, shooting star, and western tiger swallowtail butterfly

miles before draining into the dammed waters of the Columbia.

In the mountains, it is easy to imagine what this area might have looked like a hundred years ago. Large, unbroken swaths of forest blanket the countryside, and when evidence of humanity's passing is encountered, it is often in the form of an abandoned mine shaft, a decaying homestead, or a dilapidated split-rail fence. The Columbia Highlands are truly Washington's last great place, an area that has been bypassed by the urbanization and exploitation of the modern world.

A testament to a foregone era, the Columbia Mountain Lookout has graced the Kettle River Range for nearly a century. Built in 1914, it is on the National Historic Lookout Register.

Photo © Craig Romano

► An old larch tree stands guard over the San Poil River.

◄ ◄ Quaking aspen along Ninemile Creek

Natural History

Douglas squirrel
Photo © Alan Bauer

◀ Blue grouse

Words such as *awesome, stunning,* and *defiant* roll off the tongue when describing the beauty of the Cascade and Olympic mountains. The mountains of northeastern Washington rarely garner such lavish praise. Here the landscape is more likely to soothe the soul than stimulate it. While its gentle features are in marked contrast to the more dramatic scenery found west of the region, the broad diversity of ecosystems that makes up the Columbia Highlands harbors a range of flora and fauna that is rarely seen elsewhere.

The beauty in this region is subtle. It is measured in rays of sunlight filtering through a cathedral forest of ancient pines, a golden hillside teeming with deer, an alpine meadow kissed by morning dew and brushed in a rainbow of colors, or a colonnade of blue peaks fading into the night. Solace is felt in the soft breezes that whistle through shiny snags perched in heavenly gardens. The highlands are cherished for their vastness, their lack of human intervention, their rejuvenating properties, and their abundance of God's living creations.

Geology

While much of this natural canvas has been etched in smooth and soft contours, underneath the curves is a hard substructure that was created through volcanic fire and scoured by ancient glaciers and river systems. The region's geology is diverse. The eastern reaches of the Columbia Highlands consist of some of the oldest rock in the state. Once at the edge of the North American continent, the Salmo-Priest country contains sedimentary and metamorphic rock over 600 million years old. The Abercrombie–Hooknose escarpment formed 200 million years ago when colliding plates forced a coastal plain to fold and tilt upward. Abercrombie Mountain, Hooknose Mountain, and Gypsy Peak all poked above the continental ice sheets that shielded the area about ten thousand years ago. As the ice mass retreated, alpine glaciers carved steep cirques into their craggy summits.

Much of the Kettle Crest is underlaid by a granite dome that rose through the surface mantle between fifty and seventy million years ago. While most of the crest is broad with gentle slopes, the higher peaks are speckled with granite outcrops. Soil cover for much of the region is composed of thick layers of granite till left from the retreating continental ice sheets and volcanic ash cast from emerging peaks in the Cascades.

Flora

The Kettle River Range resembles the southern Appalachian peaks of Tennessee and Northern Caroline in stature, and is similarly a transition zone that is rich in plant and animal life.

In the Columbia Highlands you can hike through parklike stands of giant ponderosa pine, stately stands of old-growth Douglas-fir and grand fir, uniform stands of larch and lodgepole pine, clusters of whitebark pine and subalpine fir, and interior rain forests of western hemlock and western red cedar—all in one day.

Forest types and plant species distribution in the Columbia Highlands are greatly influenced by the west-to-east precipitation gradient. The western lowlands of the

Summer wildflower blossoms and horizon-spanning views from Abercrombie Mountain, the Columbia Highland's second-highest summit
Photo © Craig Romano

▶Summer rains freshen up the arctic lupine (*Lupinus arcticus*) and red paintbrush (*Castilleja miniata*).

Red raspberry

A slender paintbrush adds a burst of
color to the forest floor.
Photo © Jasmine Minbashian

◄ Copper Butte in summer's peak bloom

Kettles receive less than twenty inches of annual rainfall, while in the Salmo Basin,
over sixty inches of precipitation falls each year, making the area the wettest in
eastern Washington. The eastern Selkirks support moisture-laden forests of cedar,
hemlock, white pine, and yew. Stately grand fir and scaly barked Engelmann spruce
grace the Selkirk high country. Beargrass and native fescues adorn the forest floor. In
the Salmo-Priest River valley, ancient western red cedar and Douglas-fir tower over
an understory of devil's club and huckleberry. In both age and size of trees, this interior rain forest rivals its Cascades counterparts.

The western reaches of the Kettles harbor a radically different forest environment.
In the semiarid Thirteenmile Creek drainage, ponderosa pine proliferates. Some of
the state's last remaining old-growth stands of this interior northwest icon are found
in this remote and roadless valley. The dry valleys and exposed southern slopes of the
Kettles and the Midway Mountains support sprawling thickets of sagebrush. Even on

Lupine, a nitrogen fixer, grows well after intense fires.

◄ Lightning strikes at Sherman Pass

► ► Fireweed (*Epilobium angustifolium*) at sunset, from Abercrombie Mountain

the highest summits, the aromatic shrub can be found growing alongside whitebark pine and subalpine fir.

The Columbia Highlands' climate is generally continental, with cool winter months averaging 20 to 30 degrees Fahrenheit and warm summers with days often exceeding 90 degrees. However, the area is heavily influenced by maritime weather patterns. Precipitation mostly falls between October and March with another wet period in June and July. Rainfall amount, coupled with location in the transitional Inland Northwest, helps create a wide array of habitats.

The Columbia Highlands support numerous rare and sensitive plant species. In the Threemile Roadless Area, the Halliday Fen alone harbors seven state-sensitive species. Endangered sedges, moonworts, leathery grape fern, and orchids struggle to survive in wetlands throughout the region. The endemic Okanogan fameflower grows nowhere else in the world except a handful of locales in the Kettles and the adjacent Okanagan Highlands of British Columbia.

But more than rainfall, the element that has had the greatest influence on the region's flora is fire. Very few reaches of the highlands have not been touched by a great conflagration. Where fire has not descended upon the land, a climax forest of ponderosa pine, Douglas-fir, western red cedar, and subalpine fir often stands testament.

Much of the region, however, is blanketed in uniform forests of western larch and lodgepole pine, prolific pioneers of fire succession. And while these even-aged forests often don't inspire the way old-growth forests might, come autumn, the larch's delicate needles draw our admiration as they set the ridges aglow. Aspen, cottonwood, and birch add their golden touch as well.

Where fire has recently scorched the region, ghost forests haunt the slopes. But their tenure is short. Tenacious lime-green saplings crowd the charred stumps. Purple lupine, pink fireweed, and snowy-white pearly everlasting contrast nicely against the blackened logs and silver snags. Despite—and often because of—such firey interruptions, the area's forests continue to flourish.

Fauna

Hike along the lonely Shedroof Divide and count the blazes—markings left not by the ax of a trail crew but by the claws of resident bears. Trees peeled of their bark like pieces of fruit, scores of trees along the mile-high ridge display scratched trunks. If the number of defaced firs is indicative of the defacer's prevalence, it is safe to assume that a healthy black bear population inhabits these woods.

However, these bountiful bruins must share this habitat with their bigger and more elusive cousin. One of Washington's two populations of grizzly bear clings to survival in the Columbia Highlands. With an estimated population of thirty, the Selkirk grizzlies roam these highlands, migrating through the dwindling roadless areas of adjacent British Columbia and Idaho. Threatened by development, logging, and off-road vehicles, the monarch of the mountains struggles to remain a part of the greater Inland Northwest ecosystem.

The mountain caribou's existence is more precarious. Once ranging across Montana, Idaho, and Washington, the Selkirk herd is the last population of this deer family member remaining in the Lower Forty-eight. Only a few dozen survive, giving the Selkirk mountain caribou the distinction of most endangered mammal in the continental United States. Relying on a winter diet primarily of lichens and mosses growing on old-growth Engelmann spruce and subalpine fir, much of the caribou's habitat has been disturbed by logging, roads, development, and motorized recreation.

Thankfully, sufficient amounts of the Columbia Highlands have managed to escape intense development to support lynx, wolverines, and wolves. Wolverines endure in the region's boreal and subalpine forests. Lynx favor the area's large tracts of undisturbed forest, especially along the eastern slopes of the Kettle Crest. The Columbia Highlands have long been a refuge for wolves, harboring a handful as they were extirpated from most of their northwestern range. Recently, sightings of this intelligent predator have increased, suggesting that individual wolves from Canada

The yellow-headed blackbird is just one of almost two hundred species of birds that are found among the Pend Oreille National Wildlife Refuge's diverse habitats.

◄ Bighorn sheep ranged widely in the Columbia Highlands until around 1900, when disease and unregulated hunting drove them to extinction locally. In 1972, the Washington Department of Wildlife released eighteen Rocky Mountain bighorns on Hall Mountain. Today there are about sixty Hall Mountain sheep, some of which occasionally are captured and transplanted to other areas in the state.

◄ ◄ The Columbia Highlands host species more commonly found in the Rockies, such as moose, lynx, and bighorn sheep.

Photo © Alan Bauer

may be staking new territory.

The Columbia Highlands provide valuable habitat for these endangered and threatened species. But as an intact ecosystem wedged between the North Cascades and the northern Rockies, its role is magnified. Acting as a land bridge between these greater ecosystems, the region provides large carnivores a critical pathway for genetic interchange, reducing incidents of inbreeding and further helping populations to recover.

This is the only place in America where caribou, moose, elk, mule deer, and white-tailed deer cohabitate. Mountain goats and bighorn sheep, lynx and bobcat, wolf, coyote, and fox all roam the area's forests and ridges. Of the weasel family, ermine, badger, mink, wolverine, and pine marten all populate this wild corner of the state.

These wild lands support healthy avian populations, too. Bald and golden eagles, peregrine falcons, northern goshawks, and great gray owls depend on the highland's unbroken forests and undisturbed summits. The region is also home to a variety of raptors, including falcons, hawks, and eagles.

Spruce and blue grouse, three-toed and black-backed woodpeckers, white-winged crossbills, and pine grosbeaks are all a part of this special land's dynamic living tapestry. For the American redstart and the northern waterthrush, the highlands represent their only Washington distribution.

The waterways of the Columbia Highlands provide critical habitat for several endangered fish species. Cutthroat trout, Columbia Basin redband trout, and bull trout can still be found plying rivers and streams in the region.

While the Cascade and Olympic mountains contain larger ecosystems protected in national parks and wilderness areas, the ecosystems of the greater Columbia Highlands are in a way more complete, harboring more of their original inhabitants. But if we are intent on seeing that the grizzly, lynx, caribou, and wolverine remain a part of this landscape, then it is imperative that the lands they rely on for survival be permanently protected.

Human History

A three-on-three basketball tournament is one of dozens of events held during Republic's Prospector Days.

◄ Boy Scouts and American Legionnaires march in the Prospector Days parade in Republic.

Although it was the last region in Washington State to be opened to European settlement, the Columbia Highlands have long been inhabited, beginning at least after the last ice age, about nine thousand years ago. They are the ancestral lands of several First Nations: the San Poil, Colville, Okanogan, Kalispell, and (Arrow) Lakes tribes. Native peoples harvested salmon, hunted, and established trade routes throughout the region. They erected rock cairns on the high peaks of the Kettles to mark places to worship and engage in vision quests. They placed a high significance on both the healing and spiritual power of many indigenous plants.

Their first contact with Euro-Americans was in 1811, when famed explorer David Thompson, of the Northwest Company of Montreal, came to the region on a mapping expedition. Accompanied by voyageurs, Thompson traveled down the Columbia and spent time at Kettle Falls, a once-great fishery. Here the massive river crashed and churned, dropping fifty feet over a series of quartzite ledges. The hydro-

logical force was so grand that boulders bounced in the frothing waters. Thompson's French-Canadian voyageurs dubbed the cataracts La Chaudiere, meaning kettle, because it resembled a cauldron.

But more impressive than the thundering waters were the salmon runs. Hundreds of thousands of the anadromous fish passed through the falls each spawning season, providing food and barter for Native American tribes from throughout the region. They speared salmon from elevated platforms as the fish fought the rapids. Thompson's meticulous notes of the Columbia would help fuel American settlement in the region, leading to the decimation of the salmon runs and the livelihoods of the cultures that depended upon them. With completion of the Grand Coulee Dam in 1941, the falls were inundated and the salmon runs gone.

In 1825 the Hudson's Bay Company established Fort Colville on the Columbia, near its confluence with the Kettle River. Catholic and Protestant missionaries soon followed. The Columbia Highlands officially became American soil in 1846 upon signing of the Oregon Treaty. Seven years later Washington Territory was established. In 1872, President Ulysses S. Grant established the Colville Confederated Tribes, relegating the various tribes onto a 2.8-million-acre reservation extending from the Okanogan to the Columbia River.

Settlement into the region accelerated as miners, ranchers, and squatters trespassed onto Native lands. Bowing to pressure from Colville Valley pioneers, the northern half of the Colville reservation was withdrawn in 1892 by an act of Congress, reducing the reservation by 1.5 million acres. An influx of homesteaders brought an increase in ranching, lumbering, sheep grazing, and mining. Gold and other valuable minerals were discovered, fostering several boom towns.

In 1907, President Theodore Roosevelt created the Colville National Forest from remaining unsettled lands in the Columbia Highlands. (In 1942, the Tonasket District, covering the western highlands, was transferred to the Chelan National Forest, later becoming the Okanogan National Forest.) Shortly after the creation of the Colville National Forest, fire tower construction began on Columbia Mountain,

▶ The entrance to St. Paul's Mission, outside modern-day Kettle Falls

▶ *Inset:* A hunter and his "prairie chickens" at a hunting cabin near the present-day town of Curlew. The abundant bunchgrass meadows found throughout the Kettle River Range and valley are still a bird hunter's paradise.
Photo courtesy Dick Slagel

◀◀ Late-afternoon light illuminates a solid canopy of trees near Big Meadows Lake, north of Colville.
Photo © Eric Zamora

◀◀ *Insets:* Racing down the main street—with three legs or four—was a highlight of the Independence Day celebrations held in Republic around the turn of the last century.
Photos courtesy Dick Slagel

Wesley Rohr, 13, watches the competition during Prospector Days.
Photo © Eric Zamora

Local royalty wave to the crowd.
Photo © Eric Zamora

◄ Power bucking is one of many competitions of skill that takes place during Prospector Days. The contests are open to the public.
Photo © Eric Zamora

Copper Butte, Twin Sisters Butte, Mount Bonaparte, and Thirteenmile Peak, among others. To aid fire suppression, trails were constructed, but large-scale fires devastated forests throughout the region through the 1920s. In 1926, a substantial portion of Hall Mountain and the Abercrombie–Hooknose area was engulfed in flames.

The Great Depression, ironically, was a boon for infrastructure development in the Colville National Forest. Through the Civilian Conservation Corp (CCC), young men built trails, roads, campgrounds, guard stations, fire lookouts, dams, and other structures, many of which still stand today.

After World War II, the forest service increasingly took on a role as major timber supplier for local mills. By the 1960s, an emerging environmental movement, along with an influx of recreational users, often resulted in conflict with resource extractive industries. Even as the federal government passed laws aimed at balancing uses and assessing environmental impacts, timber harvesting accelerated. Competing interests frequently took their dissent to the courts, often leading to acrimonious battles.

But by the 1990s, after years of unsustainable logging and a series of federal court injunctions that forced the forest service to consider wildlife and other forest values in its management plans, timber yields were drastically cut. Along with increased mechanization and the rise of global trade favoring cheaper imports, the region's timber industry was dealt a serious blow. Mills shut down, hundreds of local workers lost their jobs, and communities throughout the highlands suffered economic hardship.

Large-scale fires swept through the area during the 1980s and 1990s, resulting in government and industry officials locking horns with conservationists over salvage logging and fire prevention policies. While over 4500 miles of roads have been constructed over the years on the Colville alone, pressure mounted to build more into large roadless areas that had been given temporary protection under the Clinton administration, further infuriating wilderness advocates. As the federal cut continued to dwindle, the forest service substantially shrunk its payroll. Suffering its own job losses, the timber industry blamed the environmental community. Conservationists blamed the timber industry, as well as the forest service, for mismanaging the national forests.

But now, after years of mistrust and bitter debate, an impasse is nearing. In this land of proud ranchers, woods workers, and others who care deeply about their local lands, longtime Columbia Highlands adversaries are beginning to realize they have much in common. Together they are finding a way to build healthy communities, foster natural resources jobs in the local economy, and protect lands, water, and wildlife—the heritage of the Columbia Highlands.

The sharpening stone is a natural landmark near St. Paul's Mission, one of the longest-occupied sites in North America. The stone is made of amphibolite, a stone more fine-grained than local bedrock, and was used by native Salish-speaking peoples for over nine thousand years to sharpen knives and spears on their way to the salmon fishing grounds.

▶ Snags are a legacy created by fire. From Edds Mountain, looking toward Thirteenmile Basin

Leaving a Legacy

Arrow-leaved balsamroot (*Balsamorhiza sagittata*)

◄ Bunchgrass meadow at the summit of Hall Mountain

The year 1984, immortalized by political satirist George Orwell, carried a bit of irony when it came to wilderness preservation in Washington State. For while politicians patted themselves on the back, and conservationists cheered over the creation of a million acres of new federally protected wilderness, few people noted that millions of acres were released from wilderness consideration—freed to be heavily logged, developed, and opened up to off-road vehicles.

In the Columbia Highlands, passage of the 1984 Washington Wilderness Bill was nothing to celebrate. Only thirty-one thousand acres of the Colville National Forest and ten thousand adjacent acres in the Kaniksu National Forest were all that were set aside as the Salmo-Priest Wilderness.

Political maneuvering by Representative Tom Foley left the Kettle River Range out of the 1984 bill. And even though the largest roadless tracts of old-growth forest and some of the best wildlife habitat remaining in northeastern Washington are in the Kettles, the future Speaker of the House chose not to protect them. The impetus behind Foley's decision remains somewhat obscure, but what is clear is the area became a sacrifice zone to intense political pressure and compromise.

The 1964 Wilderness Act was one of the boldest pieces of environmental legislation ever passed by our federal government. It specified that some lands should never be developed but should be permanently set aside as wilderness—or, as stated in the act, "an area where the earth and its community of life are untrammeled by man, and where man himself is a visitor who does not remain." Wilderness designation is the strongest protection our government may grant. It must be approved by Congress and signed by the president. Development is restricted to trails and basic backcountry amenities such as privies and signposts. Wilderness does not lock people out; it invites them to visit, but by simpler means. By foot or horseback, anyone who ventures into these sanctuaries can experience nature on nature's terms.

Not all of the national forest lands in the Columbia Highlands qualify for wilderness protection, nor should they. These forests serve other roles, too. Timber production is a valuable and viable use of our national forests. Forest products help contribute to a healthy rural economy. Recreation, too, contributes to the overall health of the local economy. Hiking, hunting, camping, skiing, fishing, horseback riding, mountain biking, snowmobiling, and foraging all have their place in the forest. Finding the right balance among all these different uses is the key to leaving a lasting legacy of wilderness, wildlife, and community.

An abandoned "wigwam" burner, which once burned sawmill waste, now sits rusting along Highway 20, east of Colville.
Photo © Alan Bauer

▶ A shaft of light from the setting sun pierces a column of rain in the Salmo-Priest Wilderness, on the borders of Idaho, British Columbia, and Washington.
Photo © Eric Zamora

A Lasting Imprint

Golden eagle

Photo © Paul Bannick

◄ Sunrise from White Mountain, an important spiritual site for local native peoples

Perhaps it was the old saying, "If you can't beat 'em—join 'em," that ushered in a new spirit of cooperation among formerly fighting factions in the Columbia Highlands. Perhaps it was the dawn of a new millennium. One thing is for certain, though: When the Northeast Washington (NEW) Forestry Coalition first met in 2002, its assortment of attendees was enough to make more than a few observers question their eyesight.

Formed to facilitate dialogue among adversarial interests regarding management of the Colville National Forest, the coalition was a bold and necessary step in trying to reach a consensus. Founded by Jim Doran, a former mayor of the Okanogan County town of Twisp, the coalition has grown to include a diverse membership. Timber mill owners (including the Vaagen Brothers Lumber Inc.), conservation leaders (including Conservation Northwest), state and federal government leaders, business owners, educators, loggers, hikers, and citizens-at-large are all active in the coalition.

The coalition's goals include restoring forests, protecting communities from wildfires, improving rural economies, and not logging old-growth and roadless areas.

The NEW Forestry Coalition has already shown that it can work together to achieve results satisfactory to all its members. The Quartzite timber sale in the Colville National Forest, just outside of Chewelah, is just one example among several that displayed how successful the coalition can be when working together with federal land managers. The coalition was able to reach a consensus to bring second-growth timber to local mills while preserving a five thousand-acre roadless tract of old-growth cedars, pines, and firs. Building off this success, the coalition has moved from identifying common ground around individual projects to finding a common vision for managing the entire Colville National Forest. After months of careful consideration and discussion, they have proposed a blueprint for a landscape-level management plan that strikes the needed balance between preserving wilderness, enhancing wildlife habitat, reducing wildfire risk near communities, and sustaining a natural resource economy.

The NEW Forestry Coalition hopes to end decades of conflict concerning forest management in the Columbia Highlands. It holds incredible potential for proposing new wilderness areas while promoting a sustainable future for the people who live, work, and play in the Columbia Highlands.

Under this new model of cooperation and trust, the possibility is real that the forces of change that threaten so much of Washington State—unbridled development and the loss and degradation of habitat—may be thwarted in the Columbia Highlands, and this timeless land and the communities within it will remain a treasure.

Participants of the Northeast Washington Forestry Coalition tour an area of the Colville National Forest that needs restoration. The coalition tour stopped for lunch at the Little Bighorn stewardship project, an experimental project aimed at using various forest treatment tactics to improve the natural environment for bighorn sheep. The project was a success, and the forest was transformed into an open, healthy, parklike stand.

Photo © Eric Zamora

▶Thunderstorm over Thirteenmile Basin

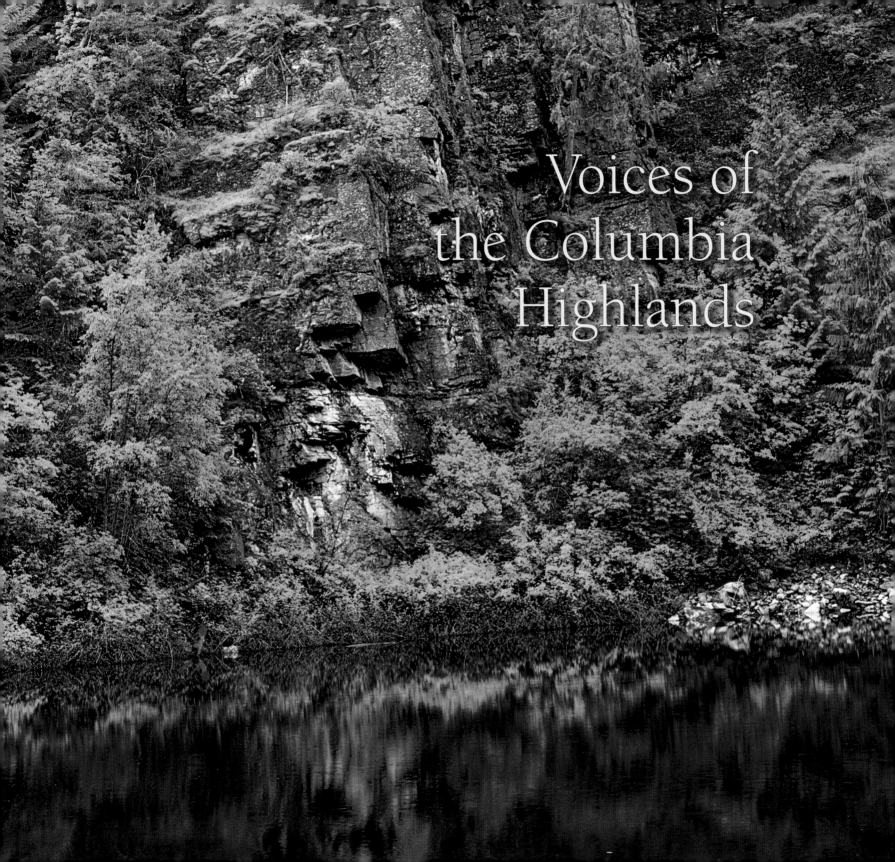

Voices of
the Columbia
Highlands

Bill Hendrix

DEER PARK

▶ Fall foliage of rose (*Rosa gymnocarpa*), thimbleberry (*Rubus parviflorus*), and currant (*Ribes cereum*) add color to a larch and Douglas-fir forest.

◀◀ Emerald Lake, Hoodoo Canyon

BILL HENDRIX HAS LIVED in Spokane County since 1971. In 1994, he moved north to the small town of Deer Park to escape the growing sprawl of the Spokane Valley. Here was more room for his horses and a better opportunity to raise his children closer to nature.

"I enjoy the outdoor life," says Bill. "Hunting, fishing, skiing and snowshoeing, horseback riding, or just picking huckleberries. There's nothing better than a nice sunny day, sitting in a huckle-berry patch, contemplating things and picking berries." It is just such a day that Bill and I enjoy while conversing over coffee on an outdoor patio in the Spokane Valley, of all places—a day better suited for enjoying and exploring the Columbia Highlands.

"I love camping at Gypsy Meadows," he continues. "It's a pleasant place…I've seen caribou up there. Another nice place I like riding is the Kettle Crest—the scenery is spectacular."

But, as he sees it, changes in the highlands could mean future losses to the places he loves. "Biggest negative impact that I've seen: more motorized use," he says. It's not so much the organized groups that are causing the problems, in his opinion, but those who are cutting their own trails, who don't seem to understand the erosion they're causing and the destruction to critical wildlife habitat.

"Another threat I see is the lack of funding from the federal government to go in and maintain these trails. I see trails deteriorating. I see locals down there with chainsaws. They say, 'The forest service doesn't care.'"

He believes, however, that the Colville National Forest is working more with user groups. "The logging industry is not as big a factor as it used to be. Communities such as Colville and Chewelah have to realize that the recreation industry is a big factor to their economy," he says, adding that preserving areas or improving trails will positively impact these communities.

"If places like Republic can embrace new wilderness areas," Bill states, "think of the jobs that'll take off—backcountry outfitters, backcountry skiing, and such."

When asked how much land should be protected, Bill says, "Make it all wilderness!" He laughs. "I am forty-something years old. I've had a good life. I've had the privilege to go out and enjoy that stuff. But you know? I want my kids—my grandkids and their grandkids—to be able to go out and see that same stuff, to be able to smell it, to feel it. It's going to take a lot of grass-roots conservation to protect it."

HORSE PACKER • MEDICAL SUPPLIES SALESMAN • FATHER OF FOUR

Old-growth ponderosa pine, a lower-elevation tree, is an increasingly rare forest type in Washington State due to logging, development, and agriculture.

Tom McKay
CURLEW

"EVERY SEASON HERE is beautiful," says Tom McKay from his home high in the hills outside of Curlew. He and his wife, Louise, came to Ferry County from Spokane in 1946. Tom was shot in the shoulder in World War II. He thought that a life in the country—farming, ranching, and sawing logs—would help rehabilitate his war injury. He built a small cabin for his family and supplemented his income by teaching in outlying towns. Now retired, he spends most of his time back on his homestead, albeit in a new home now. The original cabin still graces his property.

"Most people these days live in cities. They need a place to go out and commune with nature—see what nature is like and get an experience that you can't enjoy in the city," he says. Preserving the wilderness offers multiple benefits—not just for those who come to enjoy nature but also for those who live there. "People bring lots of money when they come here to visit. It's like hunting season: Hunting season gives Curlew a real shot in the arm. It's kind of like what Christmas is for the stores."

But Tom thinks there is another reason to protect the forests here. "The tops of these mountains shouldn't be logged," he says, because "that is where the snow cap is. It is the area that gives us water in August instead of just May and June. Without that, we are always short of water in the fall. Some places here, where there are no big trees left—why, the snow goes off it in a hurry.

"The forest service needs to be working under a leadership that has the idea of protecting the forest instead of selling the forest," he says thoughtfully. "That doesn't mean locking it up—but at least 25 to 30 percent should be wilderness. We'd be a lot better off."

It seems like a simple idea. "Protect the mountaintops," says Tom, "then you'll protect the watershed." The forest service needs to have a good long-term plan, he insists. "They should be able to log parts of the forest without denuding it. Keep a sustained yield on small areas so that there are always trees growing, always an area for wildlife, always trees for everything," he says.

FORMER FIRE FIGHTER · RETIRED TEACHER · SMALL RANCH AND WOODLOT OWNER
WORLD WAR II VETERAN · FATHER OF FOUR

Dick Vogel
KETTLE FALLS

WHETHER ON THE ROAD or on the trail, Dick Vogel has seen a lot of countryside. Arranging a meeting with Dick can be a challenge, but on a chilly November evening I was fortunate to sit down and chat with him in a hotel lobby in Colville. Dick's insights and travel tales were captivating. His genuine compassion and kindness added warmth to the frigid highlands evening.

"I hike a thousand or more miles a year—Washington, Oregon, Idaho, Montana, British Columbia, and Alaska; spectacular places like the Bugaboos, Hells Canyon, Chugach, the Bob Marshall. The Kettle Crest compares to those places," he says. "It's not as spectacular, but as an ecosystem—and a wild, beautiful, pristine, unspoiled area—I believe it's worth preserving for the plants and wildlife that live there, for human recreation, for a clean water source, for solitude."

But after living and hiking for over a quarter century in the highlands, he sees the challenges facing the region. "It's people wanting to recreate not by their own feet or on a horse but by machine," he says, shaking his head. "In the Thirteen-mile Creek area, I see motorcycle tracks going straight through beautiful meadows. It will take years to repair that."

Because of what he's seen, he says, "I would like to see the Kettle Crest and adjacent areas preserved as wilderness. We live in a wealthy country. We should ask: Is it necessary that we use every square acre to graze cattle on, to run roads into, to log? Why do we have to use every square acre for production? Why not save some of it for habitat—for the plants and animals that live there, for our own recreation, for scenic values, solitude. Preserve it for those things; they bring economy and value to the area. Without it would be like a diamond missing from its ring. That's what wilderness is—it's the diamond."

HIKER AND BACKPACKER • TRUCK DRIVER • FATHER OF THREE
HIGHLANDS RESIDENT FOR OVER TWENTY-FIVE YEARS

Ray Kresek
SPOKANE

IF ANYONE KNOWS firsthand about protecting wild lands in the Columbia Highlands, it's Ray Kresek. Ray was instrumental in helping to secure wilderness designation for the Salmo-Priest River divide in 1984. This small but important area in the Selkirk Mountains is the only protected wilderness in the highlands.

"The grizzly bear and the caribou are what sold the world on the Salmo-Priest," he says. But it took time and determination—and a lot of signatures—to save it. From his home, a living museum of Northwest fire lookout history just north of Spokane, Ray spoke of how the Salmo-Priest Wilderness came to be.

"I was hunting in the Salmo Basin in 1969 and happened to see some survey stakes way up by the cabin. I was the president of The Spokane Mountaineers at the time, and I thought, 'This needs to be wilderness.' So I used the teeth that I had with The Spokane Mountaineers to get ten thousand signatures." But that was only the beginning.

"We went to hearings in Ione, Metaline, Newport. I had two flat tires at the hearing in Metaline. It was their way of saying, 'Go away.' But I didn't go away. I had eighteen organizations behind me, from horse clubs to canoe clubs, hikers, climbers, birders."

Ray knows that much of the success in protecting the Salmo-Priest was due to various user groups—groups often in conflict with each other—coming together for a common goal. He believes any new wilderness designations will only come about if these groups can once again come together.

"One of the nice things about the Colville National Forest is that we have ponderosa pine forests. We've got white pine, we've got lodgepole pine, five varieties of firs, spruce—and you've got red cedar, too. It's a pretty diverse place. There are a lot of places in the forest that we go to that haven't changed in fifty years.

"I think the Colville has done a fair job of managing their forest, but it has been public pressure that has caused it. You've got to keep on the guard," he says. "It has always been the loggers here and the Sierra Club there. Somewhere you have to come back to the middle."

RETIRED SPOKANE CITY FIRE FIGHTER • AUTHOR, *FIRE LOOKOUTS OF THE NORTHWEST*
ORGANIZED THE DRIVE TO PROTECT THE SALMO-PRIEST WILDERNESS

🐝 Ponderosa pine forests
rely on fire to maintain
an open, grassy
understory.

Chris Jorgenson
RURAL RESIDENT

CHRIS JORGENSON cherishes his freedom and solitude. He lives with his girlfriend on the San Poil River, a long way from any town. And while he extols the virtue of living simply off the land, he is a deep thinker who understands life's complexities and interconnected-ness. For a quiet man, he can become quite extroverted if he warms up to you. On the opening day of hunting season, Chris made the trip to Republic to meet with me, a thoughtful act on one of the area's most revered days.

What makes the highlands special? "Four distinct seasons," says Chris. "It's a way of keeping time in your life without a clock." The trees, too, have made an impact on Chris. "I've been in ponderosa groves, lay-ing on my back on the beargrass, looking up through the swaying trees. The sunlight and wind and blue sky—just perfectly brilliant—and these big enormous pillars like they were supporting the sky," he says. "I don't know of any place around here that protects them, and they should be."

Changes to the area during his lifetime, he feels, have been relatively dramatic. There has been "incredible damage to the watersheds; occurrences of wildlife have been dramatically re-duced; the amount of game that I used to see on a daily basis is nowhere what I used to see," he laments. "Forest management gets a lot of attention, but I really think that livestock has done as much damage. In tandem, they're terrible," he adds.

"As a logger, what I would like to see is sustainability. Everyone uses that word—tosses it around a lot. But I know that you can't take more than what an area will support or replenish."

THIRD-GENERATION LOGGER · GREW UP IN WILBUR
FERRY COUNTY RESIDENT SINCE 1979

Dick Slagel
REPUBLIC

LIFELONG COLUMBIA HIGHLANDS resident Dick Slagel has felt an affinity toward the land since he was a child. "My awareness of the environment and appreciation of the woods and outdoors and wild places probably started when I was ten years old," recounts Dick. "Because Republic was a sleepy little town, our recreation was to get out and hike around."

He had the opportunity to travel across America as a teenager. In 1944, during World War II, he was drafted and sent to Europe as a medic. But even after seeing new lands, he was content to return to Republic. "I can remember my last furlough," he recalls. "This area looked just like heaven."

Dick's love for the Columbia Highlands became a catalyst to protect them. "My feeling has always been, well—this is my forest. I have a personal interest in it." Dick developed that personal interest during his college years. "I worked for the forest service," he says. "For several years I was on fire lookout. The last summer before I was drafted, I spent on White Mountain—it was just great. I loved that. It was quiet. You could look all around you and the forest was relatively undisturbed. It was

pretty pristine." He pauses. "It gets in your blood."

But after the war, Dick's forest was no longer a quiet place. Logging had accelerated and was threatening some of the very places Dick revered, including the Kettle Crest. In 1976 he founded the Kettle Range Conservation Group. Its main purpose was to secure wilderness protection for much of the Kettle Crest. He remembers when, back in the 1970s, the Colville National Forest's forest plans offered wilderness protection as an option. The forest supervisor at the time thought that it was a mistake. "He said he really didn't consider that 'wilderness quality,'" Dick recalls. "I remember that I told him that you don't have to have a Matterhorn in the middle of it to be wilderness quality, do you?"

Dick was devastated when the Kettle River Range was left out of the 1984 Washington Wilderness Bill. But he continues to advocate for its protection and has remained optimistic that the area will someday carry wilderness designation. "This new coalition—the Northeast Washington Forestry Coalition—is the most encouraging thing that I have seen," says Dick. "I think that it will accomplish it."

BORN JULY 4, 1919, IN REPUBLIC • WORLD WAR II VETERAN • RETIRED PHARMACIST
FOUNDER, KETTLE RANGE CONSERVATION GROUP

Geraldine Gabriel
N E S P E L E M

AFTER MEETING at the Colville Tribal Center, Geraldine and I sat and had coffee at the new community center. Surrounded by golden hills and stands of ponderosa pine, it might appear to an outsider that little has changed on the 1.4-million-acre Colville Indian Reservation since it was created in 1872 in the heart of the Columbia Highlands. But not according to Geraldine, who was born here and has lived on the reservation for over sixty-five years.

"I started riding horses when I was about three years old—rode horses just about all of my life," says Geraldine. "We would ride about ten miles out and ten miles back in all directions. To me, we're part of the land that we live on. It is a part of us.

"What I can see is that the creeks are drying up sooner," she says. "Some of the creeks are totally dry now, and other creeks are drying by July when they used to run year-round. It's affecting the whole ecosystem." She thinks clear-cutting is at fault, particularly the loss of old-growth forests that has contributed to the snowpacks melting much eaarlier than in the past.

"The logging practices here are taking too much of the old growth," Geraldine says. "They're doing helicopter logging, taking off the moun-

taintops and ridges, which is affecting not only the ecosystems but also the aesthetics of the whole region. They need to quit looking at our land as resources and dollar signs."

Cattle encroaching on watersheds is another concern. Lakes that her people have depended upon for fish and recreation are being polluted—dying, she says—because of a lack of sound management practices. Cattle contaminating the water and ruining fish beds along with an increase in sedimentation from logging debris, she says, has contributed to the dire state of the surrounding lakes. "These are the lakes that have been important to my people for generations," she says.

Geraldine thinks they should let the land come back naturally, that they should "have ceremonies to pray there and make it come back to the way it was. All of our mountains are sacred; all of our land is sacred to us. We need to protect and to preserve this land as our ancestors have done for us."

Geraldine does what she can for the land that has sustained her people for centuries. "My sister, Barb, and I are praying for them to do the right thing—to not take this land for granted."

TRIBAL MEMBER, COLVILLE NATION · MOTHER OF EIGHT

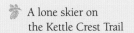

Sue Coleman
REPUBLIC

WHEN SUE ISN'T BUSY working the counter, checking inventory, or overseeing the kitchen at the Kettle Crust Bakery in Republic, she's probably out enjoying the nearby Kettle River Range. An avid backcountry skier, she was immediately attracted to the area's lofty peaks and empty slopes. She moved here with her husband, Tim, because she wanted to live a more simple life. "We were living in Portland at the time, and we felt pretty disconnected from our basic needs. The land drew us. It has never been heavily developed," she says.

But there are more people living in the county now. "The economy is a lot more stable than when we first moved here. When we first bought our property here, you could walk across Main Street blindfolded. There was hardly any traffic," she says.

And while she believes that new blood has been good for the region, she also thinks that many of those who live here now are afraid that if the government turns the area into wilderness, they'll be kept out. "There are a lot of misconceptions," she admits.

"I think many people fear change—but if we don't put some of this land into wilderness, threats in the form of resource extraction and off-road vehicle use will impact all of these people. Most people stay here because they love the land."

Sue thinks it's the land that makes the highlands a special place. "We live in a mountainous region that is very diverse. The forests just in our county alone are quite diverse. There's drier forest as well as cedar. There's a fair amount of water for eastern Washington," she says.

"My passion is skiing. I love the Sherman Pass–White Mountain area. I spend a lot of time there in the winter. I really love the whole Kettle Range—outrageous views of flowers and open meadows and sagebrush." Sue is passionate about protecting the highlands and would like to leave as her legacy a wild landscape. "I would like to know that in another hundred years people took a stand on protecting the Columbia Mountains. I hope that other people will be able to experience an unaltered landscape. Maybe even wolves will move back into the area."

MANAGER, FERRY COUNTY CO-OP (KETTLE CRUST BAKERY)
HIGHLANDS RESIDENT FOR TWENTY-FIVE YEARS

Everett Russell
REPUBLIC

A FORMER CONSTRUCTION contractor from Yakima, Everett jumped at the chance to be a full-time painter when his wife landed a job as a mental health counselor in Republic in 1988. "As an artist I can paint anywhere, but some places are much nicer than others. This is beautiful—there is literally a painting everywhere you look," Everett tells me.

We met at the Gold Mountains Art Gallery, a cooperative gallery run by a dozen artists, Everett included. The fact that Republic supports such an enterprise says something about this community. "The people by and large are quite conservative, but they're very nice," explains Everett. "They let you just be an artist. They don't think that it is strange at all."

Everett sees the pure beauty in natural landscapes. He recognizes that it is in wilderness that Nature has brushed her finest works. But he also recognizes the importance of wilderness in the sustainability of rural economies. "Wilderness is a great draw. People come here to fish and to enjoy the mountains in the summertime. They come here in the fall to hunt. They come here to savor the beauty of the country."

Everett believes that the economic future of places like Republic lies in ecotourism. "Natural resource extraction will still be a base. Logging will still continue to a certain extent; and there will still be mining as they discover more deposits," he says. "But I think that, by and large, we have to change." He points to former mining towns such as Vail, Colorado, as an example—places that have become immensely wealthy and successful by pursuing a direction away from resource extraction.

"Almost everywhere a wilderness area has been established that is within reach of tourism has benefited that community. That's true all over the western United States, and I think that creating a wilderness in the Kettle Crest can benefit Republic, Curlew, and Danville."

ARTIST OF OIL LANDSCAPE PAINTINGS · FERRY COUNTY RESIDENT SINCE 1988

John Eminger
CHEWELAH

JOHN EMINGER CONSIDERS himself fortunate because he is one of a handful of people who actually lives in the Colville National Forest. On a small inholding high in the Selkirk Mountains, John gets to look out each day at what he considers a drop-dead beautiful place. His commute to work is short—all within the Colville. On a crystal-clear late autumn day, with new snow blanketing the highlands, I traveled to John's place of work to chat with him about skiing, wilderness, and the future of the Columbia Highlands.

"I didn't buy a ski area because I hate the woods," says John. "I'm an outdoors person. I bought a ski area because I love the outdoors. Driving up here on a fall day is so reminiscent of a fall day in the Blue Ridge."

What brings John here after living all over the United States? "It's got all four seasons. I love spring the most—and of course I love winter. This area is such a beautiful spot, and you have these great rivers.

"What I've discovered in my business is that you are essentially just a caretaker of the mountain for a generation," he says. "I have this vision for the northeast corner of Washington to move away from extractive industries—at least our reliance upon them." He thinks logging and mining can be managed to work side-by-side with recreation, which relies on wilderness.

"I live here in the northeast corner of Washington," he reiterates. "I find it to be incredibly beautiful. I suppose I'd like to set aside the last wild spots for my children. I would love to have had just a small finger in having wilderness designated in the northeast corner of Washington.

"When I see these [Northeast Washington Forestry] coalition meetings and we've got these guys who have gone to war against each other in the same room, finally agreeing because something needs to be done—I derive a great deal of satisfaction from that."

OWNER OF 49 DEGREES NORTH SKI AREA SINCE 1996
GREW UP IN A NEVADA RANCHING FAMILY

Duane & Russ Vaagen

COLVILLE

THE VAAGEN BROTHERS Lumber Company, founded by Duane Vaagen's father and uncle, is an imposing landmark in the small city of Colville. Bustling with activity, this major provider of jobs in the Columbia Highlands has seen its ups and downs in over half a century of operation. Because the mill converted to smaller-diameter saws in 1996, the Vaagens have been able to continue their lumber business when many others have failed. Duane and his son Russ made time to meet with me. Their responses were both professional and savvy, delivered with anecdotes and a warm touch.

On what makes the highlands special, Duane Vaagen says, "The word that immediately comes to me is 'freedom.' If we want to take off right now for the woods, we can! It's freedom. This land is open and it's very usable.

"Of course, we just don't want to work in the forest," he continues. "We want to see the forest do well. Just because we are industry doesn't mean we care less. We're part of the solution."

"Jobs and wilderness can coexist," says Russ. "I don't think there's any question if it is done right. Wilderness and recreation jobs do not equal an economic engine to a community; they add to what needs to be an existing economic engine powered by the resources of the area," he says. "I have no doubt if there was a Kettle Mountain Wilderness, there would be people coming here to explore it because it's a wilderness—so this will bring in some economic activity."

Vice president of the Northeast Washington Forestry Coalition, Russ is happy to see that real dialogue is taking place between different user groups. "I think it's kind of refreshing that this whole thing is finally coming to fruition," says Duane. "People needed some time to digest the fact that groups that once fought with each other were now sitting together at the table. Now we've got a lot of credibility. I think there is a lot of trust built up with conservation members," he says.

"True environmentalism—the environmentalist of tomorrow, which would include us—would be promoting wood as the best possible building product because it truly is renewable, and we are utilizing methods that aren't extraction based but restoration based," says Russ. "And with that, we would be restoring communities."

DUANE:
PRESIDENT, VAAGEN BROTHERS LUMBER INC.

RUSS:
VICE PRESIDENT, VAAGEN BROTHERS LUMBER INC., AND MILL DIRECTOR

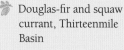

Cole Chamberlin & Sarah Iris Summy

REPUBLIC

NINE-YEAR-OLD Cole Chamberlin knows what makes his home town of Republic special. It's "the pretty views," he says confidently. But it's also what those pretty views harbor that Cole appreciates—lands that allow him to ride his bike, ski, sled, and swim.

Cole is just as certain about what is detrimental to the countryside in which he loves to play. "Tearing apart mountains to find gold," he says, is a bad idea.

The nice views and the trees should be protected, he thinks, but not just because they make his home in the Columbia Highlands pretty. "The trees let us breathe," he adds. "If I were the president I would grow more trees."

SARAH IRIS SUMMY, age twelve, thinks Republic is special because of "the nature." Like Cole, she, too, points to the abundance of outdoor activities that are available in the Columbia Highlands. "At certain times you can go fishing, swimming, hiking, hunting, skiing, sledding, and bicycle riding," she says.

She thinks the highlands should be protected. "I want them to be here forever," she states. She believes more of the surrounding forest should be off-limits to development, and that the area's wildlife needs to be better cared for. "To people who don't think this is important," she says, "I would tell them, 'Think about the future—it probably won't have as many forests.' If we protect them now, it will."

REPUBLIC ELEMENTARY SCHOOL STUDENTS

Tim Coleman
REPUBLIC

"I LOVE TO HUNT and fish," says Tim Coleman. "I love to hike, to mountain climb and ski. My favorite of all things is telemark skiing. Stationed in Japan, I started mountain climbing," he says. Tim lights up when he talks about recreating in the outdoors. Being in Japan and seeing a culture where, in his view, "they had developed everything," made him reconsider the benefits of a country where wilderness is possible. In Japan, he says, "The only thing they had left were these steep-sided mountains, and even then they tried to farm by terracing," he says. "[It] really gave me the sense of what unbridled development can do to the last wild places."

The highlands fulfill his need for wilderness. "This area has four distinct seasons and every element of the West, whether it's Arizona or the Pacific rain forest. Hoodoo Canyon is really special. It offers all these different biophysical environments, all these different forest types. You go from dry ponderosa pine, yellow balsamroot—the classic interior Rocky Mountain forest—to wet cedar forests and beautiful lakes."

On the Kettle Crest, his favorite places for hiking are the Jungle Hill and Wapaloosie trails. They combine two really special forest types—high elevation subalpine fir and sagebrush. "I mean, where do you get that mix? That is just incredible—you get the cedar, hemlock, and devil's club that you would find in the wettest forests of the Pacific."

To protect this area, he says, "You have to challenge ignorance." He thinks that is what is unique about the Northeast Washington Forestry Coalition. "It's a collaboration, bringing together the timber people with conservationists and finding that we have shared values, that we have common interests: healthy forest ecosystems."

He thinks the highlands has what it takes to mold the area accordingly. "The most important thing is the community here. The people are hardworking and caring, and they're supportive. That is what makes a good community."

"The federal lands belong to all citizens; they're not forest service lands—they're national forests. The forest service is charged with managing them. I think we're entering into a new era, but we still have old baggage that is limiting the forest service's capabilities. But we in this region are setting a new course and dragging the federal land managers along with us."

To sum up his perspective, he paraphrased one of his favorite quotes from Terry Tempest Williams: "The future is looking back at us and hoping that we care enough about them to pass on this beautiful earth in good condition."

WILDERNESS CAMPAIGN DIRECTOR, CONSERVATION NORTHWEST
FORMER NAVY CRYPTOGRAPHER

Exploring
the Columbia
Highlands

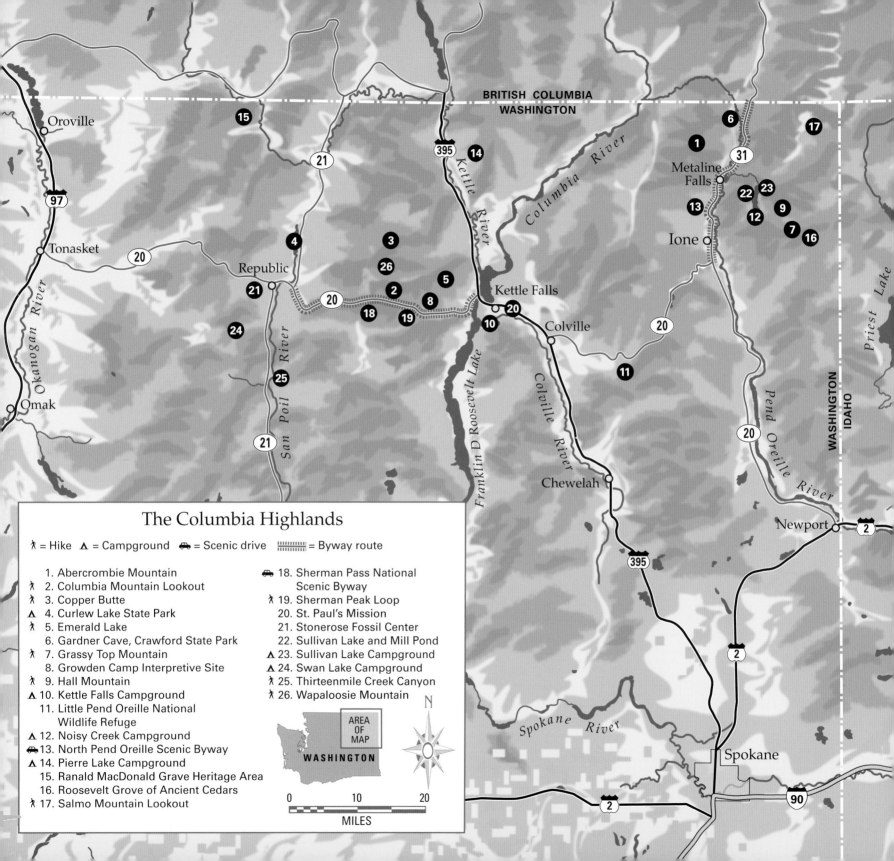

The Columbia Highlands

𝑘 = Hike   ▲ = Campground   🚗 = Scenic drive   ▥ = Byway route

1. Abercrombie Mountain
𝑘 2. Columbia Mountain Lookout
𝑘 3. Copper Butte
▲ 4. Curlew Lake State Park
𝑘 5. Emerald Lake
6. Gardner Cave, Crawford State Park
𝑘 7. Grassy Top Mountain
8. Growden Camp Interpretive Site
𝑘 9. Hall Mountain
▲ 10. Kettle Falls Campground
11. Little Pend Oreille National
     Wildlife Refuge
▲ 12. Noisy Creek Campground
🚗 13. North Pend Oreille Scenic Byway
▲ 14. Pierre Lake Campground
15. Ranald MacDonald Grave Heritage Area
16. Roosevelt Grove of Ancient Cedars
𝑘 17. Salmo Mountain Lookout

🚗 18. Sherman Pass National
     Scenic Byway
𝑘 19. Sherman Peak Loop
20. St. Paul's Mission
21. Stonerose Fossil Center
22. Sullivan Lake and Mill Pond
▲ 23. Sullivan Lake Campground
▲ 24. Swan Lake Campground
𝑘 25. Thirteenmile Creek Canyon
𝑘 26. Wapaloosie Mountain

AREA
OF
MAP

WASHINGTON

N

0   10   20

MILES

FRIENDLY COMMUNITIES, scenic drives and trails, intriguing historic and natural sites—the Columbia Highlands are a delight to explore. The region is sparsely populated but rife in adventure and surprises. The larger towns provide sufficient amenities for travelers, but don't expect to find many services in the far reaches of the highlands. Time moves slowly here. Leave the hurried life behind as you explore the Columbia Highlands.

The main towns in the highlands, which provide the bulk of lodging and dining options in the region, are also the best access points for the features found in this section. But the highland's greatest attraction is its wide-open spaces and public lands. Included here are some of the nicest campgrounds to be found among them. Various land agencies manage these campgrounds, each with their own amenities and operating schedules. Contact information for the agencies is included in the resources section at the end of the book.

It is important to note that while locater maps are provided, they do not substitute for a good Washington State highway map; be sure to carry one with you. A Colville National Forest map, available at area ranger stations, is also recommended if you travel off the main roads. If you plan to visit the Little Pend Oreille

National Wildlife Refuge, consult the refuge headquarters for a detailed map of the refuge.

Finally, additional resources are included at the back of the book, including important phone numbers and websites for tourist facilities and contact information for groups and organizations that are working to protect the highlands. You'll also find a list of other books that may prove helpful in getting to know the region.

The Columbia Highlands are an exceptionally beautiful place to explore. You won't find interstate highways here, or tract housing and strip malls flashing neon lights—the sterile landscape of much of twenty-first century America. In the Columbia Highlands you'll find an America that still embraces its past—yet holds so much promise for the future.

◄ ◄ Skiers on Bald Mountain

Republic

Founded as Eureka after an 1896 gold rush, this town of one thousand has retained much of its pioneer charm. Although it is the commercial center and seat of government for Ferry County's 7600 residents, you still won't find a traffic light in this community. Nor will you find fast-food restaurants or chain stores. Republic's main street, Clark Avenue, makes for pleasant strolling, as does Perry Wilderness Park and the paved Golden Tiger Pathway. Admire several historic structures and murals depicting the city's history. Good accommodations, art galleries, an organic bakery, and an interesting museum grace Republic.

▶ Ponderosa pine, birch, and the Kettle River

DRIVE Sherman Pass
National Scenic Byway

**SR 20, from Republic
to the Columbia River**
35 miles

Named for Civil War General William Tecumseh Sherman, who passed through the area in 1883, Sherman Pass is the highest maintained highway pass in Washington State. Retracing a historic Native American trade route, this thirty-five-mile scenic byway traverses the Kettle River Range via the 5575-foot pass.

Start your journey on SR 20 in the old gold mining town of Republic and drive east. Wind your way through the Colville National Forest to Lake Roosevelt, the massive 130-mile-long body of water created on the Columbia River by the Grand Coulee Dam. Pass through the stark landscape left by the 1988 White Mountain Burn—over 20,000 acres of forest were scorched by a lightning storm. Enjoy a picnic or night under the stars at Sherman Overlook, perched high on the Kettle Crest. Then follow Sherman Creek through a lush forest of larch, Douglas-fir, and ponderosa pine. In autumn, marvel at the emerald canopy streaked with gold, thanks to thick stands of larch. Admire tumbling falls along Sherman Creek. Watch for beaver and moose in marshy spots along the way. Relive history at Growden Camp Interpretive Site, an old CCC camp. Visit an early twentieth-century log flume. Gaze out at Lake Roosevelt's azure waters from the grassy, rolling hills of the Sherman Creek Wildlife Area.

EXPLORE Stonerose Fossil Center

Located just in the Republic city limits, the Stonerose Fossil Center includes an interpretive building and an outdoor fossil digging site. Visitors may pay a minimal fee and, under curator supervision, dig for fossils at the large shale deposit hillside. Impressions of plants, insects, and fish over fifty million years old have been excavated at the site. These fossils hold many clues to deciphering the geologic and biologic past of the region. Several of these historic testaments are on display at the small interpretive center located across from the Republic City Park.

EXPLORE Ranald MacDonald
Grave Heritage Site

This state heritage site in the Kettle River Valley, about ten miles west of Curlew, commemorates the life of adventurer Ranald MacDonald. Born in Astoria, Oregon, to a pioneer Scotsman and Chinook princess, MacDonald learned Japanese at Fort Vancouver. He successfully entered Japan (which was closed to foreigners at the time), where he taught English and promoted an open relationship between the Japanese and the Americans. Admiral Perry's successful

negotiations with the Japanese were a result of MacDonald's prior work. After extensive travel, MacDonald lived out his life in Ferry County.

CAMP Curlew Lake State Park
Washington State Parks

Nine miles north of Republic, on SR 21

Once the summer camp of local Indian tribes, this 123-acre state park makes a nice base for exploring the Columbia Highlands. Choose from eighty-two sites, including a handful overlooking the five-mile-long lake. Utility hookups and hot showers are available. Enjoy trout or bass fishing, or explore the park's shoreline nature trail.

CAMP Swan Lake Campground
Colville National Forest

Fourteen miles south of Republic, on FR 53

Swan Lake is a quiet little campground in the southwest corner of the Colville National Forest that offers twenty-five well-separated sites, many with views of the little lake. There is good swimming as well as hiking from the campground. Ferry, Fish, and Long lakes are nearby. Admire the CCC-built picnic shelter, and let the resident loons serenade you with their eerie calls.

Coyote, Copper Butte burn
Photo © Alan Bauer

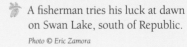
A fisherman tries his luck at dawn on Swan Lake, south of Republic.
Photo © Eric Zamora

Kettle Falls

Located on a broad bluff above Lake Roosevelt, present-day Kettle Falls was first known as Myers Falls. The original Kettle Falls town site, along with its namesake, was inundated in 1939 when the Columbia River was dammed. Myers Falls, however, still flows, but it has been altered to produce hydroelectric energy. Kettle Falls once supported a magnificent run of salmon. An interpretive center at the falls, along with a replica of a gristmill, is an interesting diversion. The Kettle Falls Historical Center, which has documented over 9000 years of human history in the area, is also worth visiting. Camping and boating are popular at nearby recreation areas.

Goatsbeard leaves (*Aruncus dioicus*)

◀ Ponderosa pine needles

EXPLORE St. Paul's Mission

Two miles west of present-day Kettle Falls is St. Paul's Mission. Under the guidance of Jesuit missionary Father Anthony Ravalli, Native Americans constructed a hand-hewn log church here in 1846. St. Paul's served the community until the 1880s. Reconstructed in 1939, the mission is now a monument to the mission era of the Northwest frontier. Located on a bluff at the confluence of the Columbia and Kettle rivers, it is part of the Lake Roosevelt National Recreation Area. An interpretive trail leads a quarter of a mile around the grounds.

EXPLORE Growden Camp Interpretive Site

The Growden CCC Camp is one of several historic sites along the Sherman Pass National Scenic Byway (SR 20). The Civilian Conservation Corp (CCC) was commissioned in 1933, under President Franklin D. Roosevelt, to put young men to work in the nation's national parks and forests. From Growden, also known as Little America because its enrollees represented many areas of the country, workers constructed trails, roads, camps, and fire lookouts throughout the Colville National Forest. Not much of the camp remains—just foundations and interesting interpretive signs—but its legacy lives on throughout the Colville National Forest.

CAMP Kettle Falls Campground Lake Roosevelt National Recreation Area

Three miles west of Kettle Falls, on Boise Road

This popular campground occupies the original Kettle Falls town site on the Columbia River. A one-mile interpretive trail weaves through foundations and orchards of the old town. The falls were inundated with the building of the Grand Coulee Dam. The campground contains seventy-six sites and a large boat-launching area.

Colville

With just under 6000 residents, the city of Colville is the largest community in the Columbia Highlands. Colville is the Stevens County seat and the major commercial and transportation center for the region. The administrative office for the Colville National Forest is located here, and forest products manufacturing accounts for a significant portion of the city's economy. Colville is situated in a wide valley surrounded by forested mountains. Its lovely scenery, coupled with its wide range of services and streets lined with charming historic Victorian homes, make Colville a pleasant vacation spot. The Keller Heritage Center, with its museum, fire lookout, old schoolhouse, and pioneer cabins, is of particular interest. Colville is also home to a thriving arts community.

The White Mountain fire burned forty thousand acres in 1988, leaving behind only toothpick snags and burgeoning new growth, like this summer-blooming lupine.

Photo © Eric Zamora

EXPLORE Little Pend Oreille National Wildlife Refuge

Another legacy of the Depression Era, the Little Pend Oreille National Wildlife Refuge (NWR) was formed from the acquisition of abandoned farmland in the hills and valleys east of Colville. Today the Little Pend Oreille NWR protects nearly 42,000 acres of wildlife habitat, sporting healthy populations of white-tailed deer, black bear, and turkey. Hunting is permitted, and several refuge lakes are open to fishing. Hiking is allowed on the refuge's primitive roads, and camping is permitted at designated areas. There also is good bird watching here, especially during the spring months.

CAMP Pierre Lake Campground Colville National Forest

Thirty-five miles north of Colville, on County Road 4015

This small campground (fifteen sites) is on a remote lake in a quiet section of the Colville National Forest. A one-mile trail hugs the shore, providing access to fishing spots and wildlife observation. The tranquil lake makes for good canoeing.

Chewelah

Chewelah occupies the southern end of the wide and scenic Colville Valley. The economy of this city of 2200 traditionally was dependent on resource extraction. Forest products still make up an important part of Chewelah's workforce, but the 49 Degrees North Ski Area increasingly has played a stronger role in the area's economy. Located ten miles east of the city on Flowery Trail Road, 49 Degrees North recently increased its skier capacity and terrain. Chewelah's downtown area retains an early twentieth-century atmosphere. Several historic buildings sport new businesses. The Chewelah Museum houses a large collection of area photographs.

Snags near Snow Peak, on the Kettle Crest Trail

Ione

This little town of 450 residents is the largest settlement in northern Pend Oreille County. Although Ione's main employers are manufacturers of forest products, tourism has steadily been gaining importance. Situated on the Pend Oreille River and within easy access to several lakes, Ione is a supply center and base for boaters, anglers, and paddlers. The North Pend Oreille Valley Lions Club operates a charming old train several times a year that takes tourists on a scenic excursion along the Pend Oreille River and through Box Canyon.

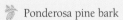
Ponderosa pine bark

◀ Bighorn sheep
Photo © Alan Bauer

EXPLORE North Pend Oreille Scenic Byway

SR 31, Tiger to the Canadian border
Twenty-seven miles

The Pend Oreille River flows northward in Washington State. Along a wide and scenic valley, it cuts through the Selkirk Mountains to meet the Columbia in Canada. Named by early French-Canadian trappers after the Native peoples of the region who wore large pendants from their ears, the Pend Oreille once posed great difficulty for those who plied it. But dams have now stilled the waters that early nineteenth-century explorer David Thompson found challenging, and a modern state highway now allows access to a once-foreboding canyon.

Begin your Pend Oreille odyssey in the little settlement of Tiger, just south of Ione, where a 1912 store and post office is all that remains in the once-bustling commercial district. Follow the river north through more historic settlements. Admire not only their cultural significance but also their pastoral backdrops of lofty green peaks. Look for moose, bighorn sheep, bear, and deer along the way. The formerly gritty town of Metaline Falls, about ten miles south of the Canadian border, has been transformed into an arts center. Be sure to visit the Cutter Theatre here, a nationally registered historic site. Crescent Lake, not far from the border, offers weary travelers a peaceful picnicking spot, while nearby Sullivan Lake invites them to spend the night.

CAMP Noisy Creek Campground Colville National Forest

Eight miles east of Ione, on Sullivan Lake Road

This small nineteen-site campground is on the southern tip of Sullivan Lake. Amenities include a quiet beach and access to the Sullivan Lake shoreline trail and the Noisy Creek Trail to Hall Mountain.

Metaline Falls

Situated on the banks of the Pend Oreille River and surrounded by lofty peaks, Metaline Falls, population 250, is one of the most scenic communities in the Columbia Highlands. Home to a cement plant for ninety years, this once-dusty little town has transformed itself into an arts center. It recently was ranked as one of the one hundred best small arts towns in America. The old cement plant still stands, along with a dozen other historic structures, including the 1906 Washington Hotel and the 1912 Cutter Theatre. The theater, designed by renowned architect Kirtland Cutter, features a library, historic displays, an art gallery, and live performances.

▶ Metaline Falls and the Pend Oreille River, seen from Washington Rock

Photo © Eric Zamora

EXPLORE Sullivan Lake and Mill Pond

Tucked in the northeast corner of the Colville National Forest, Sullivan Lake is one of the largest natural lakes in the Columbia Highlands. Only a handful of cabins grace its nine miles of shoreline. A four-mile hiking trail runs along its eastern shore, connecting two attractive lakeside campgrounds. Forests of birch and hemlock give the lake a northern Appalachian feeling. Less than a mile downstream from Sullivan's outlet is the Mill Pond Historical Area. Here, remnants of a four-mile-long wooden flume as well as early twentieth-century structures can be viewed. A barrier-free trail provides access. Moose frequent the pond, and the area is a prime spot for bird watching.

EXPLORE Gardner Cave, Crawford State Park

Just above the Boundary Dam on the Pend Oreille River and straddling the Canadian Border is forty-nine-acre Crawford State Park, home to Gardner Cave. Extending over a thousand feet, this subterranean landmark is the third-longest limestone cave in the state. Adorned with stalactites, stalagmites, rim stone pools, and flow stone, Gardner makes for a great introduction to the underworld. With a colorful history (it was founded by a bootlegger) and features carrying imaginative names such as Packrat Nest, Fried Eggs,

and Christmas Tree, Gardner is a fun place to explore. Park rangers lead tours from late April to early September.

EXPLORE Salmo Mountain Lookout

From this fire tower lookout, perched 6828 feet above sea level, is an eagle's eye view of the 41,335-acre Salmo-Priest Wilderness, the only federally protected wilderness in the Columbia Highlands. The lookout can be reached by driving FR 22 east from Sullivan Lake for six miles. Go east on FR 2200 for twelve miles to spur road 270. Follow spur road 270 for two miles to its end. The current lookout was built in 1964 and staffed until 1976. It is one of only a handful of lookouts still remaining in the Columbia Highlands. Enjoy good berry picking and excellent views of the Salmo-Priest River Basin and Gypsy Peak, the highest mountain in eastern Washington.

EXPLORE Roosevelt Grove of Ancient Cedars

Located within the cool and lush Granite Creek Valley is an old-growth grove of western red cedar that may have you thinking that you're in the Cascades. Over fifty inches of rain falls annually in this far corner of the Washington Selkirks, helping to explain the presence here of such a fine stand of cedar. Named in honor of President Theodore Roosevelt and designated a scenic area by the Kaniksu National Forest in 1943, the ancient

cedar grove contains trees that are over 2000 years old. Reach this primeval forest via Idaho SR 57 from Priest River to Nordman, Idaho, and then continue twelve miles north on FR 302. Or from Sullivan Lake follow FR 22 east for twenty-two miles, which becomes FR 302 just over Pass Creek Pass.

CAMP Sullivan Lake Campground
Colville National Forest

Seven miles east of Metaline Falls, on Sullivan Lake Road

One of the prettiest campgrounds in the state, family-friendly Sullivan Lake is divided into two areas and offers forty-eight large, forested, private sites, all within walking distance of a sandy beach on the lake. There is a four-mile shoreline trail. Sullivan Lake is a good base for exploring the nearby Salmo-Priest Wilderness.

Although most of the Roosevelt Grove of Ancient Cedars was destroyed by fire in 1926, the remaining twenty acres are virgin, which means the trees have never been cut. The cedars are between four and twelve feet in diameter and range in age between eight hundred and two thousand years old.

Photo © Eric Zamora

Newport

The Pend Oreille County seat and commercial center, this little town of 2000 makes for a charming stop. Originally founded in Idaho, Newport was rebuilt across the state line after an 1894 fire. Its rich transportation history is told in the historic artifacts of the town's river-running and railroad days, which can be viewed at Centennial Plaza. Adjacent is the Pend Oreille County Historic Museum, housed in an old depot. Newport's downtown invites pleasant strolling, while the nearby Wolf Donation Trails double as a mountain bike and Nordic ski center. Several lakes grace Newport's outskirts and offer plenty of paddling and camping opportunities.

The first snowfall of winter coats the golden grasses on Wapaloosie Mountain.
Photo © Jasmine Minbashian

◄ Ponderosa pine trunk

Hiking the Highlands

Columbia Mountain Lookout

ROUND TRIP: 8 miles

ELEVATION GAIN: 1200 feet

TRAILHEAD: Marked trail at Sherman Pass on SR 20, seventeen miles east of Republic

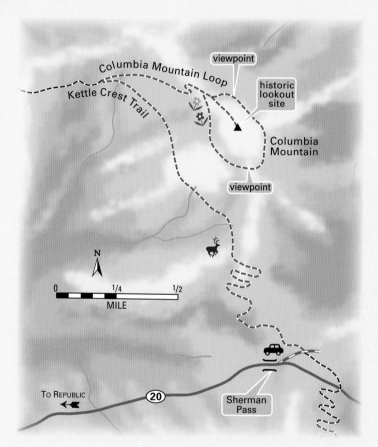

Wander trails through high-country meadows flush with flowers. Gaze upon sweeping views of the Sherman Creek Valley, the unbroken swaths of forest that cloak King Mountain and the Twin Sisters, and hillsides that are hopping with deer. Visit an historic fire lookout cabin that has graced this Kettle Crest summit since 1914.

From the large parking area on Sherman Pass, follow the Kettle Crest Trail north for two miles to the Columbia Mountain Loop Trail. Turn right and, after half a mile of climbing, come to another junction. Go left or right—it doesn't matter; the two-mile loop just below the summit yields knockout views in every direction no matter what direction you march off in.

Be sure to take the half-mile marked spur to the 6780-foot summit of Columbia Mountain. Emerge on the broad open summit with its weather-beaten and element-defying lookout cabin, built during the Wilson administration. It would be fitting if this testament of the golden age of conservation could stand watch over a Kettle Mountain Wilderness.

Beargrass (*Xerophyllum tenax*) on Cromwell Ridge, Salmo-Priest Wilderness
Photo © Charles Gurche

Sherman Peak Loop

ROUND TRIP: 5.3 miles

ELEVATION GAIN: 900 feet

TRAILHEAD: Marked trail at Sherman Pass on SR 20, seventeen miles east of Republic

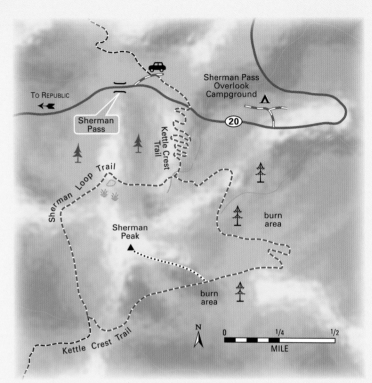

This hike offers striking views of a landscape struck by the forces of nature. The loop takes you on a full-circle tour around 7011-foot Sherman Peak, revealing the mountain's two contrasting sides: a forest of lush green old growth, and one scorched by wildfire that resulted in a surrealistic landscape of silver snags.

Head south on the Kettle Crest Trail. Cross SR 20 and start ascending. Under a cool canopy of larches, fir, and pine, the trail twists and turns out of Sherman Pass. Come to the loop junction and bear left. Skirt beneath a steep hillside of ledge and scree. Stop for a breathtaking view of Sherman Creek Valley.

At about a mile, enter a radically different world, thanks to the White Mountain Fire of 1988, which seared over 20,000 acres of Kettle Crest greenery. Through the skeletal remains of what was once a verdant forest, continue climbing.

As you round the pyramidal summit of Sherman Peak, signs are all around that the forest is coming back to life. A new row of greenery is slowly filling in the silver snags and hollow logs, creating a diverse forest important to wildlife.

Reach a junction and return right on the Sherman Loop Trail. Like the landscape that you're traversing, mature forest is once again reached.

Wapaloosie Mountain

ROUND TRIP: 6 miles

ELEVATION GAIN: 2000 feet

TRAILHEAD: On Albion Hill Road (FR 2030), 3.3 miles
from its junction with SR 20 (4 miles east of Sherman Pass)

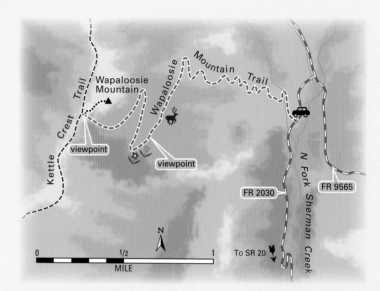

*One of the highest summits on the Kettle Crest, 7018-foot Wapaloosie
Mountain offers extensive views and some of the finest alpine meadows
in the Columbia Highlands. Thanks to a southeastern exposure, the trail
melts out by late spring. This trail traverses one of the region's most
dramatic plant communities: slopes of sage brush interspersed with
groves of pine and fir.*

*Hike Wapaloosie early in the season to experience its bounty of blos-
soms. As soon as the snow melts, arrowleaf balsamroot speckles the
mountainside bright yellow. Arnica, yellow violet, and mountain dan-
delion follow. Alpine lupine eventually takes over, punctuating the soft
greens and yellows of the sedges and grasses with shades of violet.*

Start through a uniform stand of lodgepole pine, the quintessential
interior-montaine forest. In a mile, break out of the canopy to begin
your odyssey across Wapaloosie's sprawling meadows. Views are
far-reaching, ranging from British Columbia's Rossland Range to the
Abercrombie–Hooknose highlands. Mack and King Mountains stand out
like emerald sentinels, guarding the eastern flank of the Kettle Crest.

Aster, lupine, fireweed, yarrow, and paintbrush create a mosaic of
colors across the meadows. Buckwheat, hawkweed, rabbit brush, and
spirea crowd the sagebrush that creeps toward the summit.

Reach the Kettle Crest Trail in 2.75 miles. Venture along the crest
through an open forest of whitebark pine and subalpine fir, or take a
side trip with an easy ten-minute ascent from the junction through
more meadows to Wapaloosie's broad and open summit.

Copper Butte

ROUND TRIP: 9.5 miles

ELEVATION GAIN: 2400 feet

TRAILHEAD: From SR 21 just north of Republic, follow County Road 284 (Fish Hatchery Road) about three miles to Echo Bay Mine. Now follow FR 2152 east for three miles to FR 2040. Bear left and at five miles from the junction with FR 2152 turn right on FR 250. In 1.5 miles more find the trailhead, on the left.

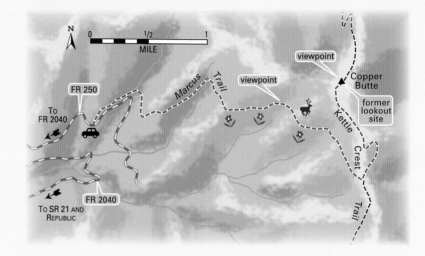

At 7140 feet, Copper Butte is the highest summit in the Kettle River Range. Of several ways to reach this lofty peak, no route is as beautiful as the Marcus Trail. By way of this lightly traveled trail you'll walk through old-growth, fire-succession, and subalpine forests as well as some of the most prolific alpine meadows within the entire range.

Begin in an open forest of giant ponderosa pines and Douglas-fir. After half a mile, enter a large area that succumbed to a fire in the early 1990s. By early summer, waist-high fireweeds bombard the burn with a profusion of purple. You'll soon reenter a mature forest of fir and larch. In two miles the trees yield to hundreds of acres of resplendent meadows. In early summer enjoy a dazzling floral show of bistorts, lupines, yarrows, roses, golden peas, asters, buttercups, locoweed, bluebells, and paintbrush.

At 3.5 miles is an intersection with the Kettle Crest Trail, in a high saddle along the ridge. Turn left and head north for 1.25 easy miles to the summit of Copper Butte. Once home to a fire lookout, horizon-spanning views still remain of the Cascades and Idaho's Selkirks, Mount Spokane, and British Columbia's Rossland Range.

Thirteenmile Creek Canyon

ROUND TRIP: 8 miles

ELEVATION GAIN: 2000 feet

TRAILHEAD: On SR 21, twelve miles south of Republic at the Colville National Forest–Colville Indian Reservation border

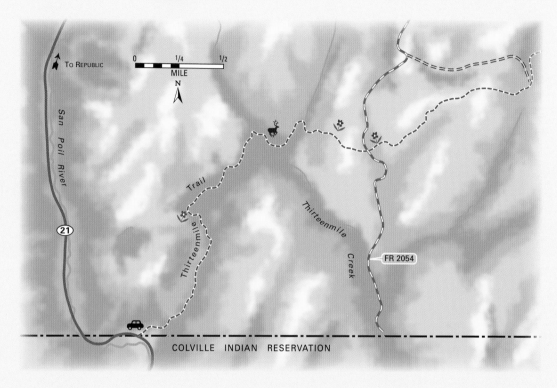

The Thirteenmile Trail ventures 16.5 miles through some of the loneliest and most spectacular country in the Columbia Highlands. Traversing terrain encompassing rugged ridges, sprawling alpine meadows, and a steep-walled canyon, the Thirteenmile Trail takes adventurous hikers into a little-explored and little-known region of the Kettle River Range. But it is not necessary to hike this challenging trail in its entirety to experience the beauty and remoteness of this region.

The first few miles of trail pass through a narrow canyon flanked by towering granite walls and graced with stately groves of giant old-growth ponderosa pines. In springtime a carpet of wildflowers brightens the canyon's floor, while eagles and hawks ride thermals looking for bounty. Cougars make themselves at home in the canyon, and chances are good of spotting a black bear and plenty of mule deer.

After about 2.5 miles the trail climbs out of the canyon, reaching a forest service road in four miles. The trail continues for twelve more miles, skirting the summit of Thirteenmile Mountain and crossing the high saddle between Fire and Seventeenmile mountains.

Emerald Lake

ROUND TRIP: 6.2 miles

ELEVATION GAIN: 650 feet

TRAILHEAD: At milepost 337 on SR 20, between Republic and Kettle Falls, head north on FR 020. Drive for five miles to Trout Lake and the trailhead.

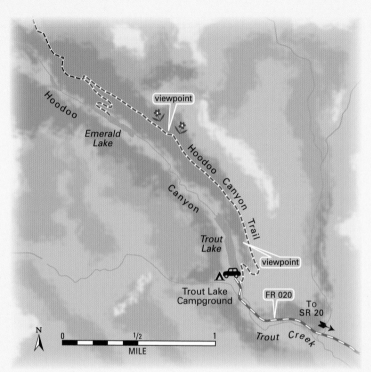

Emerald Lake is located in the heart of the steep-walled, glacially carved Hoodoo Canyon. The hike to this little gem is short, but you can easily spend all day in the canyon. The trail begins at pretty Trout Lake, at the head of the canyon.

Start in a cool forest of cedar and fir, cross the outlet of Trout Lake, and immediately begin to climb. At first your surroundings are quite lush; the trail plows through a forest of salal, snowberry, current, thimble-berry, maple, birch, and dogwood. But as you switchback out of the damp canyon floor to a ledge along the canyon wall, a new landscape emerges—one with greater exposure to the sun.

Traverse across the sun-baked eastern wall of the canyon. Giant ponderosa pines provide some shade. After two miles, Emerald Lake comes into view far below in the canyon. A short descent begins across an open, grassy shelf, providing precious warmth in early season or brutal heat come July.

The junction with the Emerald Lake Trail is just beyond. Turn left. In just over half a mile and 200 feet in elevation loss, you'll arrive at the shores of the lake at the bottom of the canyon. Let your mood dictate the plan. Explore nearby boulder fields, take a cooling dip, or sit and reflect by the quiet waters.

Abercrombie Mountain

ROUND TRIP: 6.5 miles

ELEVATION GAIN: 3220 feet

TRAILHEAD: From Colville, follow Aladdin Road north for 27.5 miles. Turn right on Deep Lake–Boundary Road and continue for 7.25 miles. Turn right on Silver Creek Road (FR 7078). In 2 miles bear left. In 4.4 miles turn right on FR 300. The trailhead is in 3.5 miles, at road's end.

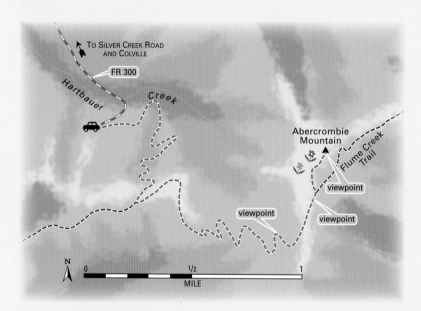

The second-highest peak in eastern Washington, Abercrombie Mountain offers sweeping views from the Cascades to Idaho's Selkirks, from British Columbia's Monashees to its Purcells, from the Pend Oreille River to the Columbia River, and from British Columbia's Kootenay Valley all the way to the Columbia Plateau. But if the panoramic vistas don't woo you, the alpine meadows exploding with wildflowers will.

The trail begins on an old logging road. Follow this alder-lined path for 1.4 miles. Turn left at a junction and, after a few steep sections, break out of the forest canopy to the swaying grasses and vibrant blossoms of Abercrombie's high country.

At three miles is the junction with the Flume Creek Trail. Continue left for a quarter of a mile, making one last climb to the rocky summit, where you will find a monster cairn and the ruins of an old fire tower. But they won't hold your attention for long; the views scream out. The Kettle Crest dominates the western horizon, while directly east, the emerald ridges and craggy peaks of Salmo-Priest country rise a mile above the placid Pend Oreille Valley.

Grassy Top Mountain

ROUND TRIP: 8 miles

ELEVATION GAIN: 1000 feet

TRAILHEAD: From Metaline Falls, follow Sullivan Lake Road east for 4.75 miles. Turn left (east) onto FR 22 and proceed for 13.75 miles to the trailhead, at Pass Creek Pass.

This is one of the easiest ridge hikes in the Columbia Highlands. The effort to reach 6253-foot Grassy Top may be minimal, but the payoff is grand. Magnificent meadows and splendid views of the Salmo-Priest country await you.

Starting with a little drop, the trail enters a cool, old-growth forest of spruce and fir. Angling around a scattering of ledges, the way begins to ascend via a series of long and gentle switchbacks. After 1.5 miles the brunt of the climb is complete. It is now a pleasurable hike along a ridge that hovers between 6000 and 6200 feet. In 2.7 miles is a junction; go left. Soon the trail enters an expansive meadow carpeted in wildflowers. If the ending seems anticlimactic, retrace your steps for five minutes or so to find an unmarked trail that takes off to the north from the main trail. This short, steep path climbs 200 feet to a 6375-foot knoll. The views here are even better than from the main summit, especially north, to the Salmo-Priest country.

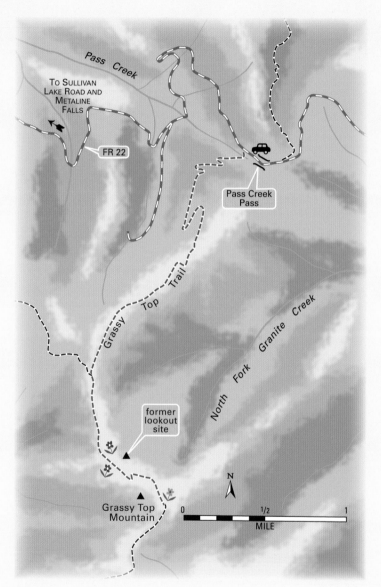

Hall Mountain

ROUND TRIP: 5 miles

ELEVATION GAIN: 1000 feet

TRAILHEAD: From Metaline Falls, follow Sullivan Lake Road east for 4.75 miles. Turn left (east) onto FR 22 and proceed for 3 miles. Turn right onto Johns Creek Road (FR 500) and continue for 7.5 miles to the trailhead.
Note: The road is subject to closures for wildlife management. It is usually open from July 1 to August 14. Check with the Sullivan Lake Ranger Station at (509) 446-7500 before visiting.

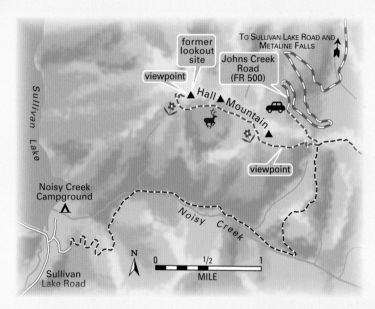

Hall Mountain is a prominent peak in Washington's Selkirk Mountains. Towering above sparkling Sullivan Lake, Hall's wide-open alpine meadows provide not only knockout views of the pristine lake far below but also prime habitat for a band of bighorn sheep. Deer, elk, cougar, and black bear also call this lofty mountain home, and a few wayward grizzlies have trampled Hall's swaying grasses from time to time.

Begin with an easy hike of just over half a mile to a four-way junction. The left trail heads over lonely terrain to Grassy Top Mountain. The trail straight ahead plunges into the deep cool forests of the Noisy Creek Valley to emerge at Sullivan Lake. The trail to the right—the one to take for this hike—climbs 700 feet in just under two miles to Hall's 6323-foot summit. From this former fire tower lookout site, embrace the breathtaking views of the deep, green Sullivan Valley and the rugged Crowell Ridge that rises behind it.

Look, too, for evidence of Hall's wild denizens. And if the mountain's mega-fauna doesn't make itself seen, its mega-flora will. A mosaic of multihued blossoms and meadows carpet the mountain.

Acknowledgments

Writing this book is in many ways reflective of protecting the Columbia Highlands. First there was a vision; then it took a diverse and committed group of people to make it happen. I could not have completed this work without the support and cooperation of so many committed individuals.

I am deeply grateful to my publisher, Helen Cherullo, of the Mountaineers Books, for bringing me into this project and believing in my work. I am also indebted to my editor, Christine Clifton-Thornton, for all of her hard work, support, and encouragement on this book. Your mimosas are on the way!

A special thanks to Jasmine Minbashian and all of the folks at Conservation Northwest for also believing in me. It was a real honor to work with you. I have been a member almost since the organization's inception (back when it was the Greater Ecosystem Alliance; I still have a vintage tee shirt with the old logo that I proudly wear). I feel that this book is my greatest contribution to helping protect our special Northwest wild lands.

I couldn't possibly have completed this book without Conservation Northwest's Tim Coleman. Tim, you have always been a world of knowledge on the region, and your compassion and commitment to protecting it is contagious. I have enjoyed all of our conversations over the years and appreciate all of your help.

Thanks, too, to photographer James Johnston. James, it was great traipsing around

A male western bluebird prepares to leave his nest in a burned birch after delivering food to his young.

Photo © Paul Bannick

◀ Bald Mountain at sunset, from the Snow Peak shelter near the Kettle Crest Trail

Ferry County and the Colville Indian Reservation with you. It was also nice to share hiking stories with someone else who loves the Kettles as much as I do.

I am greatly appreciative of all the people who contributed their time for interviews for this book. Thank you, Derrick Knowles, for helping arrange some of those interviews. Thanks also to Evelyn Adams for the use of Jim Hays' beautiful line drawings.

I want to thank my wife, Heather, for being so supportive and patient with me as I worked on the manuscript. And thanks, Heather, for not being too jealous when I went off wandering the Columbia Highlands without you. I know how special this area is to you as well—and I wish you were able to accompany me on each and every hike.

Lastly, I wish to dedicate this book to Gary Wilson. The first time I ever set foot in the Kettle River Range, it was with you, my friend. I'll always cherish the fond memories I have of us hiking to Columbia Peak in the fog and camping at Curlew Lake on a warm summer night, and the thrill of exploring a new region together. I know that you are in a place more beautiful than the Columbia Highlands now. I am glad we were able to share so many wonderful times together, including "discovering" this special corner of God's beautiful planet.

Cones of Douglas-fir, grand fir, and Engelmann spruce

Freckle pelt lichen (*Peltigera aphthosa*), found in the temperate rainforests of the Selkirk Mountains, provides winter forage for mountain caribou.
Photo © Jasmine Minbashian

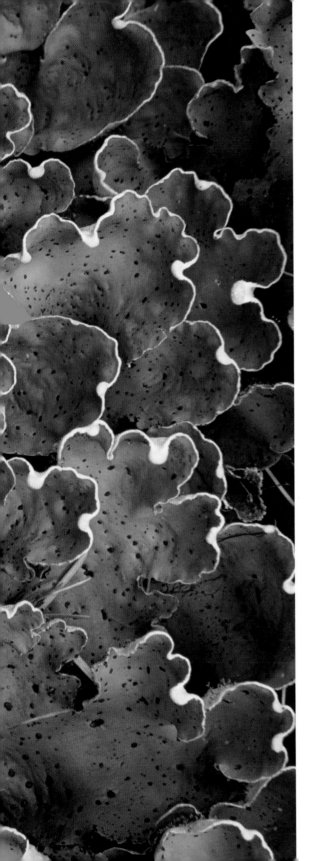

About the Author

CRAIG ROMANO was raised in New Hampshire, where he fell in love with the natural world. He has traveled extensively, from Alaska to Argentina, Bulgaria to South Korea, seeking wild places. He ranks Washington State, his home since 1989, among the most beautiful places in the world. The Columbia Highlands he finds especially magical for their remoteness, biological diversity, and raw beauty.

An avid hiker, runner, kayaker, and cyclist, Craig has written about his passions for many publications, including *Backpacker, Canoe and Kayak, Northwest Travel, Northwest Outdoors, AMC Outdoors, The North Columbia Monthly,* and *Northwest Runner.* He also writes recreational content for Canada's *theweathernetwork.com* and for *Hikeoftheweek.com.* He coauthored *Best Hikes with Dogs: Inland Northwest* with Alan Bauer and is author of *Day Hiking: Olympic Peninsula.* He also contributed to *Best Wildflower Hikes: Washington.*

He holds an associate's degree in forestry, a BA in history, and a graduate degree in education. He teaches part-time in the Edmonds and Shoreline (Washington) school districts and works part-time in Europe's Pyrenees Mountains as a guide for Walking Softly Adventures. In August of 2006, Craig married his beloved Heather at Curlew Lake State Park in the Columbia Highlands.

Oak ferns (*Gymnocarpium dryopteris*)

About the Photographers

JAMES JOHNSTON is a native Oregonian who lived in Washington State during 2005 and 2006 while completing the photography for this book. He is an avid hiker, backpacker, fly fisherman, and photographer who has covered more than a thousand miles of trail in the Pacific Northwest every year since he was old enough to drive. He currently lives in Eugene, Oregon, with his life partner Zella, a red-haired Rhodesian Ridgeback. More of his photography can be found at *www.northforkphotos.com.*

PAUL BANNICK is an award-winning natural history photographer who has been featured in books and magazines including Sunset and Pacific Northwest Magazine. *www.paulbannick.com*

ALAN L. BAUER is a professional freelance photographer and a lifelong resident of the Pacific Northwest who specializes in natural and local history. *www.alanbauer.com*

CHARLES GURCHE is a professional photographer who has produced over 15,000 images. His work has appeared in a wide range of books, magazines, and calendars including National Geographic Society and national parks publications. *www.charles-gurche.com*

JASMINE MINBASHIAN has visited all seven continents to photograph wild landscapes, including Antarctica, Patagonia, and the Russian Arctic, but she regards her home in the Pacific Northwest as the most beautiful place on earth. *www.jasminemin-bashian.com*

ERIC ZAMORA is a freelance photojournalist from Florida who discovered the Columbia Highlands while working with photographer Art Wolfe on two projects exploring wilderness and community in the West. *www.ericzamora.com*

Beargrass
Photo © Paul Bannick

Resources

Legislative Contacts

Representative Cathy McMorris
1708 Longworth House Office Building
Washington, DC 20515
(202) 225-2006
fax: (202) 225-3392
mcmorris.house.gov

Senator Maria Cantwell
Washington, DC, Office
717 Hart Senate Office Building
Washington, DC 20510
(202) 224-3441
cantwell.senate.gov/contact/

Senator Patty Murray
Washington, DC, Office
173 Russell Senate Office Building
Washington, DC 20510
(202) 224-2621
murray.senate.gov/contact/

Land Managers

Colville Confederated Tribes
PO Box 150
Nespelem, WA 99155-0150
(509) 634-2200
www.colvilletribes.com

Colville National Forest
Main Office
765 South Main Street
Colville, WA 99114
(509) 684-7000
www.fs.fed.us/r6/colville

Washington State Department
   of Natural Resources
Commissioner of Public Lands
Department of Natural Resources
PO Box 47001
Olympia, WA 98504-7001
(360) 902-1004
cpl@wadnr.gov
www.dnr.wa.gov

Ranger Districts

Newport Ranger District
515 North Warren
Newport, WA 99156
(509) 447-7300

Republic Ranger District
650 East Delaware Avenue
Republic, WA 99166
(509) 775-7400

Sullivan Lake Ranger District
12641 Sullivan Lake Road
Metaline Falls, WA 99153
(509) 446-7500

Three Rivers District
Kettle Falls Office
255 West 11th Street
Kettle Falls, WA 99141
(509) 738-7700

Other Resources

Chewelah Chamber of Commerce
204-A East King Street
PO Box 94
Chewelah, WA 99109
(509) 935-8991
info@chewelah.org
www.chewelah.org

Colville Chamber of Commerce
121 East Astor Street
Colville, WA 99114
(509) 684-5973
colvillecoc@plix.com
www.colville.com

Crawford State Park
General Delivery
Metaline Falls, WA 99153
(509) 446-4065
www.parks.wa.gov

Curlew Lake State Park
974 Curlew State Park Road
Republic, WA 99166
(509) 775-3592
www.parks.wa.gov

Ferry County Chamber of Commerce
   and Visitor Information Center
PO Box 91
Malo, WA 99150
(509) 779-4808
www.ferrycounty.com/files/visitorinfo.html

Ione Chamber of Commerce
PO Box 549
Ione, WA 99139-0549
(509) 442-4010
http://www.wcce.org/city.htm

Kettle Falls Chamber of Commerce
PO Box 119
Kettle Falls, WA 99141-0119
(509) 738-2300
www.kettlefalls.us

Lake Roosevelt National Recreation Area
1008 Crest Drive
Coulee Dam, WA 99116
(509) 633-9441
www.nps.gov/laro

Little Pend Oreille National
   Wildlife Refuge
1310 Bear Creek Road
Colville, WA 99114
(509) 684-8384
www.fws.gov/littlependoreille/

Metaline Falls Chamber of Commerce
PO Box 388
Metaline Falls, WA 99153-0388
(509) 446-4012
www.wcce.org/city.htm

Newport/Oldtown Chamber
   of Commerce
325 West 4th Street
Newport, WA 99156
(509) 447-5812
chamber@conceptcable.com
www.newportoldtownchamber.org

North Pend Oreille
   National Scenic Byway
PO Box 603
Ione, WA 99139
www.byways.org/browse/byways/2233/
www.povn.com/byway/

Republic Regional Visitors
   and Convention Bureau
Gateway to Adventure
979 South Clark Avenue
PO Box 325
Republic, WA 99166
(509) 775-3387
www.republicwa.com

Sherman Pass National Scenic Byway
PO Box 91
Malo, Washington 99150
(509) 779-4808
www.byways.org/browse/byways/2232/

Stonerose Interpretive Center
   and Eocene Fossil Site
15 North Kean Street
Republic, WA 99166
(509) 775-2295
srfossil@rcabletv.com
www.stonerosefossil.org

Tiger Historical Center
PO Box 603
Ione, WA 99139
(509) 442-0288

Conservation, Forestry, and Recreation Organizations

Conservation Northwest
600 South Clark, Suite 7
Republic, WA 99166
(509) 775-2667
info@conservationnw.org
www.conservationnw.org

Faith and Environment Network
1620 North Monroe Street
Spokane, WA 99205
(509) 329-1410
environment@interfaithnw.org

Hunting and Fishing Conservation
   Coalition
1224 2nd Street
Cheney, WA 99004

Inland Northwest Trails Coalition
35 West Main, Suite 220
Spokane, WA 99201
www.inlandnorthwesttrails.org

The Lands Council
423 West 1st Avenue, Suite 240
Spokane, WA 99201
(509) 838-4912
tlc@landscouncil.org
www.landscouncil.org

The Mountaineers
300 Third Avenue West
Seattle, WA 98119
(206) 284-6310
www.mountaineers.org

Northeast Washington Forestry Coalition
PO Box 262
Colville, WA 99114
(509) 684-5071
www.newcommunityforestry.org

Sierra Club
Upper Columbia River Group
10 North Post Street, Suite 447
Spokane, WA 99201
(509) 456-8802
idaho.sierraclub.org/uppercol/

The Spokane Mountaineers
PO Box 1013
Spokane, WA 99210-1013
(509) 838-4974
www.spokanemountaineers.org

Recommended Reading

Bamonte, Tony, and Suzanne Schaeffer Bamonte. *The History of Pend Oreille County.* Spokane, WA: Tornado Creek Publications, 1996.

Bamonte, Tony, and Suzanne Schaeffer Bamonte. "Pend Oreille County," in *Pathways to History: Roads, Trails and Journeys, the Mingling of Peoples and the Forming of Northwest Communities.* Spokane, WA: Tornado Creek Publications, 2005.

Bragg, L. E. *A River Lost.* Blaine, WA: Hancock House, 1995.

Dietrich, William. *Northwest Passage: The Great Columbia River.* New York: Simon & Schuster, 1995.

Kettle River History Club. *Reflections of the Kettle River Region.* Republic, WA: Kettle River History Club, n.d.

Johnson, James P. *50 Hikes for Eastern Washington's Highest Mountains.* Portland, OR: Frank Amato Publications, 2003.

Lakin, Ruth. *Kettle River Country: Early Days Along the Kettle River.* Orient, WA: Lakin, 1976.

Landers, Rich. *100 Hikes in the Inland Northwest.* Seattle, WA: The Mountaineers Books, 2003.

Mueller, Marge, and Ted Mueller. *Exploring Washington's Wild Areas,* second edition. Seattle, WA: The Mountaineers Books, 2002.

 Rufous hummingbird at red-flowering currant

Lupine foliage

Nicholls, Dennis. *Trails of the Wild Selkirks South of the Canadian Border.* Sandpoint, ID: Keokee Books, 2004.

Nisbet, Jack. *Visible Bones: Journeys Across Time in the Columbia River Country.* Seattle, WA: Sasquatch Books, 2003.

Nisbet, Jack. *Mapmaker's Eye: David Thompson on the Columbia Plateau.* Pullman: Washington State University Press, 2005.

Perry, Madilane. *A Brief History of Ferry County.* Republic, WA: Ferry County Historical Society, 1994.

Romano, Craig, and Alan L. Bauer. *Best Hikes with Dogs: Inland Northwest.* Seattle, WA: The Mountaineers Books, 2005.

Walter, Edward M., and Susan A. Fleury. *Eureka Gulch: The Rush for Gold.* Colville,WA: Don's Printery, 1985.

Northern saw-whet owl
Photo © Paul Bannick

▶ Douglas-fir and squaw currant

Index

 Lupine grows alongside a ponderosa pine tree.

Photo © Eric Zamora

THE MOUNTAINEERS BOOKS
is the nonprofit publishing arm of The Mountaineers Club,
an organization founded in 1906 and dedicated to the exploration,
preservation, and enjoyment of outdoor and wilderness areas.
1001 SW Klickitat Way, Suite 201, Seattle, WA 98134

Printed in China

Editor: Christine Clifton-Thornton
Acquiring editor: Helen Cherullo
Cover design: Nancy Duncan
Book design and layout: Jane Jeszeck/www.jigsawseattle.com
Illustrator: Jim Hays, © Evelyn Adams
Cartographer: Gray Mouse Graphics
Photographer: © James Johnston unless noted otherwise

Cover: *Looking west at sunrise from the Salmo Mountain fire tower, Salmo-Priest Wilderness*, Eric Zamora. Insets: *Grizzly bear cub*, Paul Bannick; *Old barn, Little Pend Oreille National Wildlife Refuge*, Alan Bauer; *Arrow-leaved balsamroot*, James Johnston; *Stella Runnels, of the Colville Confederated Tribes, Nespelem*, James Johnston. Back cover: *Sunset from Copper Butte*, James Johnston. Half-title page: *Mountain lady's slipper*, Eric Zamora; frontispiece: *Sunset and wildflower meadow, Salmo-Priest Wilderness Area*, Charles Gurche; title page: *A common loon tips its bill among yellow waterlilies (Nuphar polysepalum)*, Paul Bannick; page 5, top: *Ponderosa pine needles*, bottom: *Pileated woodpeckers on a ponderosa pine tree*, Paul Bannick.

A Note About Safety

Safety is an important concern in all outdoor activities. No book can alert you to every hazard or anticipate the limitations of every reader. Therefore, the descriptions of roads, trails, routes, and natural features in this book are not representations that a particular place or excursion will be safe for your party. When you follow any of the routes described in this book, you assume responsibility for your own safety. Under normal conditions, such excursions require the usual attention to traffic, road and trail conditions, weather, terrain, the capabilities of your party, and other factors. Keeping informed on current conditions and exercising common sense are the keys to a safe, enjoyable outing.

The Mountaineers Books

Library of Congress Cataloging-in-Publication Data

Romano, Craig.
  Columbia Highlands : exploring Washington's last frontier / text by Craig Romano ; photos by James Johnston. — 1st ed.
    p. cm.
  Includes bibliographical references and index.
  ISBN 0-89886-816-5 (alk. paper)
1. Uplands—Washington (State) 2. Uplands—Washington (State)—Pictorial works. 3. Columbia Plateau Region—Description and travel. 4. Rocky Mountains Region—Description and travel. 5. Cascade Range Region—Description and travel. 6. Washington (State)—Description and travel. 7. Natural history—Washington (State) 8. Washington (State)—Environmental conditions. 9. Environmental protection—Washington (State) I. Title.
F897.C7R66 2007
979.7--dc22

                    2006037540

 Printed on recycled paper

The Columbia Highlands Initiative

In October of 2005, Conservation Northwest launched its Columbia Highlands Initiative, a local cooperative effort to identify a common vision for managing the Colville National Forest that sustains jobs, restores forests, protects wildlife and wilderness, and ensures outdoor recreation opportunities for all. The initiative includes a campaign to designate wilderness areas in the Kettle River Range and the Selkirk Mountains.

CONSERVATION NORTHWEST protects and connects old-growth forests and other wild areas from the Washington Coast to the British Columbia Rockies, vital to a healthy future for us, our children, and wildlife. Since 1989, Conservation Northwest has worked to find solutions that are grounded in science while maintaining a common interest with rural communities. Supported by 5000 members, Conservation Northwest's staff combines science, policy, communications, and organizing skills with passion and innovation to achieve success for conservation.

www.conservationnw.org

THE MOUNTAINEERS, founded in 1906, is a nonprofit outdoor activity and conservation club, whose mission is "to explore, study, preserve, and enjoy the natural beauty of the outdoors...." The club sponsors many classes and year-round outdoor activities in the Pacific Northwest, and supports environmental causes through educational activities, sponsoring legislation and presenting educational programs. The Mountaineers Books supports the club's mission by publishing travel and natural history guides, instructional texts, and works on conservation and history.

Send or call for our catalog of more than 500 outdoor titles:

The Mountaineers Books
1001 SW Klickitat Way, Suite 201
Seattle, WA 98134
(800) 553-4453
mbooks@mountaineersbooks.org
www.mountaineersbooks.org